I0167496

LEADING
on the
PROPHETIC
EDGE

BY

DR. RUSS MOYER

McDougal & Associates is an organization dedicated to the spreading the Gospel of the Lord Jesus Christ to as many people as possible in the shortest time possible.

Published by:

McDougal & Associates
18896 Greenwell Springs Road
Greenwell Springs, LA 70739
www.thepublishedword.com

ISBN: 978-1-950398-00-3
eBook 978-1-7770528-5-2

Printed on demand in the U.S., the U.K. and Australia
For Worldwide Distribution

Presented To:

_____

By:

_____

On:

_____

Message:

_____

_____

_____

_____

Foreword by Dr. Fred L. Bennett

Dr. Russ Moyer's latest book, *Leading on the Prophetic Edge*, gives us insight into the type of leadership he employs in Eagle Worldwide Ministries. For over a year I have witnessed firsthand this leadership style that is both unique and challenging. It is a style of leadership that has successfully planted numerous churches, a Retreat and Revival Centre, the Spirit Ministries Training Centre, the Kingsway Blessing Centre and a growing network of ministries and ministers based in Ontario, Canada.

Dr. Russ knows what he is talking about concerning leadership, as he has led others for nearly forty years in sports, business and ministry. He has a strong working knowledge of the principles, skills and personal discipline needed to lead effectively. What sets him apart from so many others is how he gives priority to the Holy Spirit's leading.

This unique leadership style is a discipline that Dr. Russ holds himself to, no matter how long it takes or how much others may pressure him to short circuit the process. Since Dr. Russ has a strong and highly developed prophetic gift, he is truly running to his strength in leadership.

Many who seek to be led by the Holy Spirit give priority to circumstances, reason and wisdom, and then they look to the Spirit for guidance and confirmation. Dr. Russ has it the other way around. He begins with prophetic revelation and resists making any move or decision until he has it!

We have all said from time to time that we are being led by the Spirit, but we would be hard pressed to describe how that works for us. What Dr. Russ has practiced he now shares in this book with all who seek to be Spirit-led in whatever field of endeavor God has called them to. *Leading on the Prophetic Edge* is a must read for all who aspire to be more effective leaders.

Dr. Fred L Bennett
Ambassador to Canada
Host of The Bridge

Dedication

I would like to dedicate this book to the many leaders and mentors in my life who were willing to sow into me and believe in me, even when it was difficult for me to believe in myself:

- To the late **Anthony Chiccino.** He was my high school football coach and had a fatherly role in my life from the time I was ten.
- To **Pastor Paul Wetzel** of Pensacola, Florida. He taught me many things about life and leadership in the church and is still my pastor today.
- To the late **Ruth Heflin.** I was privileged to spend the last year of her life under her leadership at Calvary Pentecostal Campground in Ashland, Virginia, where I was mentored in my prophetic gift and calling.
- To my father, **Russell S. Moyer, Sr**. He did not have a great deal of formal education, but he was a wise man with a great street sense and he taught me more about people than I could have ever learned in some of the greatest educational institutions of this world.

I would also like to dedicate this book, *Leading On the Prophetic Edge,"* to **my spiritual sons and daughters** who have been so faithful to accept the torch and run the race. Some of them I coached in athletics, others are from my many years in business and, of course, all of those who have labored with me at Eagle Worldwide Ministries.

Parenting is one of the greatest training fields for leadership, so I also want to dedicate this to **my own children—Russell S, Moyer, III and Melissa Wilkerson.** Mave and I have four children and ten grandchildren between us, and we are believing God for His blessings to pass from generation to generation.

Acknowledgments

I would like to acknowledge the wonderful people who have partnered with me in the writing of this book, *Leading on the Prophetic Edge:*

- I want to give special acknowledgment to **my wife, Mave**, who is a constant support and co-leader with me at the helm of many apostolic and prophetic works. She puts her hands to the plow and also her faith into action and is a tremendous leader in her own right.
- Special thanks to **Miguel Simon** who designed the cover as well as formatted the original book. As Vice President of Eagle Worldwide Ministries, he helps me with a great number of projects and is a faithful son.
- **Patty Thorpe**, the Administrator at Eagle Worldwide Ministries, helped me a great deal in the clerical work and preparation for the book, particularly for the teachings I shared with the Covenant Leadership group and the monthly Prophetic Edge teachings. She has been a real spiritual daughter to Mave and me,

and a vital key to the growth and development of Eagle Worldwide Ministries.

- **Nellie Balandowich** has worked closely with me in these last two books with compiling, formatting and editing my spoken messages.
- A special thanks to **Victoria Grassick** who has most graciously edited all of our books. You are indeed a tremendous asset.

The tireless efforts of all of these in the midst of their busy schedules were an inspiration to me. In this way, we partner and share in the harvest. All of them are a tremendous blessing and wonderful to work with. They provoke me to be a better person, a better leader and a man of character. May God bless each one of them!

Endorsements for
LEADING ON THE PROPHETIC EDGE

"*Leading on the Prophetic Edge* is written by a true apostolic and prophetic leader. Russ Moyer knows what he is talking about from a biblical and experiential perspective. His prophetic gifting is a fresh revelation for God's people who want to be on the leading edge of what He is saying and doing with the present-day Church. This book will help you to manifest greater success through your gifting and God-given assignments. It's a must read for everyone!"

John P. Kelly
Convening Apostle, ICA
(International Coalition of Apostles)
Visionary Founder, LEAD
(Leadership Education for Advancement and Development)

"If there is one thing we need today, it is leadership with a prophetic edge. What would happen if you made every decision and were precisely motivated by the leading of the Holy Spirit? Dr. Russ Moyer's very timely book on leadership focuses on proven principals, timely wisdom and offers revelatory insight from the heart of a successful leader. His practical strategies and prophetic solutions can uncover the greatness in every reader who's willing to learn! If you are a leader, looking for a seasoned mentor in business or ministry, I highly recommend this book to you. Through these pages you will uncover the avoidable pitfalls and be encouraged to step into the fullest blessings that are accessible to you, while developing leadership skills that could otherwise take a lifetime to learn. This book challenges you to go beyond yourself and into the success and prosperity that's discovered by being led by the Spirit. I loved reading this important book, and I believe you will too!"

Joshua Mills
Keynote Conference Speaker and Bestselling Author
New Wine International

"The times we live in require a lifestyle of not only accurate prophetic gifting but also developing a culture of prophetic people. Russ Moyer has a real ability to raise up and release people on the prophetic edge who are trained to change the communities they live in. This book is literally a handbook on how to confidently move in spiritual maturity, while demonstrating the Kingdom of God in practical ways. Filled with keen insight and teaching, *Leading on the Prophetic Edge* will provoke you to action and energize your life and ministry."

Charlie Robinson
Revival Canada Christian Ministries

"I am so thankful for the ministry and life of Dr. Russ Moyer. I have observed his leadership and found it to be graced with seasoned wisdom, steered by divine revelation and backed up by godly character. He is tried, tested and true! This book is so clearly a reflection of all the above. I personally appreciated the nuggets I gleaned from it. Thank you, Dr. Russ, for your commitment to seeing leaders in the Body of Christ go from strength to strength and lead on the edge!"

Faytene Grasseschi
Best Selling Author, Activist and Revivalist
The CRY Canada & MY Canada

"In the general Christian market today, there are many books on leadership. They range from highly dictatorial to passively mild. Few, however, incorporate the three elements of our life as men and women who desire to see significance as an integral part of who we are. Those elements are: Christian life principals, business or economic life principals and ministry life principals. Of course, there is really only one life principal and that is to be a follower of Christ. But when you can draw on all the aspects and experiences that the Holy Spirit has guided you through, you then have a dynamic basis from which to impart to others.

"Russ has incorporated very solid teaching in this book that can help chart your life course and keep you from much pain. I heartily recommend it. Leadership is taught, caught and imparted as you hear the voice of a man who not only knows the principles but also walks them out on a daily basis.

"You may be thinking that there are other books out there that project these same characteristics, but there are elements that make this book very unique and one that will help you no matter what stage of your Christian walk you find yourself in. I call it the 'voice side.' Within the pages of this book, you will continually hear the voice of the prophet, one who thinks like, talks like and acts like a biblical prophet. When this 'voice side' is mingled with solid practical teaching, you have a book that will touch, not only your intellect, but also your heart."

George Woodward
Israel's Peace Ministries

"True leadership begins in the heart. Jesus said, *'Come and follow Me,'* and this is the essence of this cutting-edge book on leadership! There is a desire in the hearts of many believers to finish well. Dr. Russ writes about leading with an excellent spirit. There is a cry in the hearts of a generation that says, 'Lead us on.' And there are many people who are asking, 'Will you show us the way?' Russ Moyer is one of the fathers to this generation who can say, 'This is the way to walk and lead by faith.'

"This book will stir you to lead by example in your area of influence: family, church, business and community. It will help you walk in God's plan for your life and avoid some of the pitfalls along the journey of faith. There is a new way of leading: 'taking it to the prophetic edge.' May you be empowered by the Spirit of wisdom (knowing what to do) and the Spirit of might (the ability to carry it out) as you find the 'know how' to lead through the principles contained in this book. *Leading on the Prophetic Edge* is a key leadership book for a key season!"

Brent Sloss
Senior Pastor, Word of Life Regional Church

"Truly the greatest need in the world today is strong, disciplined leaders. Dr. Russ Moyer is a leader of leaders. Russ has raised up leaders in both the business world and in the Church. This book is a hands-on guide to assist you in becoming a better leader. Many practical and proven tools are in these pages, to motivate you and challenge you to cultivate solid leadership principles. I highly recommend this book to every leader and emerging leader."

John Irving
Senior Pastor, The Gathering Place

I have no greater joy than to hear that my children are walking in the truth.

3 John 4

Contents

Introduction

I hope you enjoy reading this book, *Leading on the Prophetic Edge*, as much as I have enjoyed putting it together. Learning, living and walking it out ... , there is nothing I appreciate more than the opportunity to work with leaders and emerging leaders.

I knew early on in life that there was something about me, something on the inside of me, that caused me to lead. It was almost as if I could hear a sound that caused me to think for myself and not just blindly follow others.

In my athletic career—as a football player, baseball player and wrestler—I was a leader. I played football until I was twenty-six. I was captain of my team (a semi-pro team in Pennsylvania) and ultimately a player-coach. I also coached high school football for six years and was an umpire, a referee and the president of a youth sports league in my hometown of Bridgeport, Pennsylvania, all before I reached the age of twenty-five.

Shortly after that, through dreams and visions and inspirations in my heart from God, I started my own business in the basement of my house with a few friends and less than five hundred dollars in the bank. Despite my lack in business education, finances and experience, for twenty-one years I had a wonderful and very successful time leading in the business community. Before I was finished, I had five different companies with more than two hundred employees.

I had my own weekly TV show and was honored for "leadership in business" and "working with young people" by two Chambers of Commerce and The U.S. Congress and Freedoms Foundation at Valley Forge.

In 1997, I sold my businesses and went to Bible School and then into full-time pulpit ministry. As a prophetic missionary to Canada, I pioneered eight churches in Ontario and founded and presided over Eagle Worldwide Ministries, which provides covering and apostolic oversight, not only for our own churches, but for others as well. We have several hundred ministers who have now come under the Eagle Worldwide Network. John Kelly and C. Peter

Introduction

Wagner and the International Coalition of Apostles commissioned me in my apostolic calling in 2005.

In this book I talk about the many methods and modes of learning which I have gathered from other people, my personal quest for specialized education and my pursuit of excellence. Much of what you are about to read came from personal experience. This is not something you would get at the Harvard School of Business. It comes, rather, from the place where the rubber meets the road, the place where leaders are forged, in the furnace of affliction, by trial and tribulation. Hopefully you will be able to avoid some of the pitfalls I encountered along the way.

You can certainly learn through formal education (and I have a great respect for it), and you can certainly learn through personal experience. Many are the lessons of leadership that we learn through trial and error. To me, it has also always been a seed of wisdom to learn through the errors of others.

More than anything else, I hope that *Leading on the Prophetic Edge* challenges you to go beyond yourself, to live and lead on the edge, the prophetic edge, leading at the speed of change and on the edge of chaos, not just by the seat of your pants, but by divine inspiration and the Spirit of Wisdom that can only come from above.

I wrote this book for all who aspire to spiritual or religious leadership, but I am certain that its principles can be applied to business, personal life or community life as well. Using them will help you achieve the success you were destined for.

I want to challenge you today, as you read this book, to live life to the fullest. The Lord came that we might have life and have it more abundantly. Not just life, but abundant life. I believe the heartcry of our society today is calling forth leaders of honor, integrity and morality, leaders willing to stand up for what they believe in.

I have thoroughly enjoyed the quotes of two of our most powerful leaders in the U.S.: Presidents Harry S. Truman and Franklin D. Roosevelt. Truman said, "The buck stops here." Roosevelt said, "I would rather try with all my might and fail miserably than to be found sitting on the sidelines of life with those poor souls who have never tasted victory or defeat."

More than anything else, to me, the most important thing that I can do is to raise up leaders. That is my heart: to raise up, to empower and equip leaders into their destiny. May this book be a means to that end.

Russ Moyer
The U.S. and Canada

Chapter 1

Living and Leading on the Prophetic Edge

Habakkuk 2:1-5, KJV

I will stand upon my watch, and set me upon the tower, and will watch to see what he will say unto me, and what I shall answer when I am reproved.

And the LORD answered me, and said, Write the vision, and make it plain upon tables, that he may run that readeth it. For the vision is yet for an appointed time, but at the end it shall speak, and not lie: though it tarry, wait for it; because it will surely come, it will not tarry.

Behold, his soul which is lifted up is not upright in him: but the just shall live by his faith. Yea also, because he transgresseth by wine, he is a proud man, neither keepeth at home, who enlargeth his desire as hell, and is as death, and cannot be satisfied, but gathereth unto him all nations, and heapeth unto him all people.

As I mentioned in my last book, *Living On the Prophetic Edge*, this phrase means living by faith. I am talking about the prophetic edge, the apostolic, the breaker anointing, taking it to the limit, living, ruling and reigning in the fullness of the Spirit, knowing the power and authority that has been given to us and taking it to the edge, to the limit, for the Kingdom; to extend and advance that Kingdom.

In verse 4, Habakkuk declared, *"The just shall live by his faith."* Paul wrote to the Corinthian believers: *"For we walk by faith not by sight"* (2 Corinthians 5:7, KJV). Often this seems like the most outrageous thing we could possibly do. But God will take each of us—you and me included—to a place of living on the edge if we are willing to go there.

When the Lord saved you and called you, it was not for a mediocre life of simply warming a pew or for living the *status quo*. His love for us and His plans for us are much greater than that. I love what His Word tells us in Jeremiah:

Jeremiah 29:11

> *"For I know the plans I have for you," declares the* LORD, *"plans to prosper you and not to harm you, plans to give you a hope and a future."*

It requires a lifetime of learning to hear God's voice and obey Him when He speaks, for His ways are not our ways. His ways are much higher. He therefore calls us to go up, to go beyond the veil, to learn to live and lead on the edge of chaos, managing at the speed of change.

This is not about demographic studies or charts and graphs which you can turn to and mold and turn upside down. To me, it's all about getting into the visionary realm and being led by the Spirit.

God's Word shows us:

Proverbs 29:18, KJV

> *Where there is no vision, the people perish, but he that keepeth the law, happy is he.*

This scripture reveals a simple truth, a spiritual law. Spiritual laws govern the spiritual realm just as natural or scientific laws (such as Gravity, Inertia and Relativity) govern the natural realms. Our ignorance or indifference to a natural or spiritual law doesn't change the fact that there is a cause and effect related to our activity in that realm.

The visionary realm is the prophetic realm of the Spirit and one of the ways that the Lord uses to speak to His creation. It's all about Romans 8:14:

> *For those who are led by the Spirit of God are the children of God.*

In typical business concepts, you look at key success factors, factors central to your organization and goals correctly identified and skillfully executed. Then, you come into alignment with the market's criteria for success. With me, it is all about being in alignment with the Spirit. Many times this means going against the *status quo* and the accepted protocol for operating your business (as a lawyer, an accountant or a market expert, etc.). With us, it is learning to be obedient to the still, small voice within.

Father, I pray for those whose desire is to live life on the edge in their faith, that their faith would so increase, that they would know without a doubt that they are the true

26

sons and daughters of the Lord, those who are being led by the Spirit.

Lord, I pray that the ears of their heart and spirit would be open to hearing Your voice and Your voice alone.

I pray that we would be willing to go to the edge and beyond, knowing that You will never let go of us, You will never abandon us or forsake us. You will complete every work which You have begun in us and bring us to a place of excellence to lead others.

I pray that You will give each reader Your supernatural abundant grace to dare to believe ALL that You have for them in this very time and in this very season. Lord, that each person would learn to lead on the edge, the prophetic edge!

In Jesus' name,
Amen!

THE GREAT COMMISSION OF MATTHEW 28 IS NOT TO MAKE CONVERTS BUT RATHER TO MAKE DISCIPLES!

Chapter 2

Identifying Emerging Leaders

Ephesians 4:13-15, KJV

> *Till we all come in the unity of the faith, and of the knowledge of the Son of God, unto a perfect man, unto the measure of the stature of the fulness of Christ: that we henceforth be no more children, tossed to and fro, and carried about with every wind of doctrine, by the sleight of men, and cunning craftiness, whereby they lie in wait to deceive; but speaking the truth in love, may grow up into him in all things, which is the head, even Christ.*

As a leader, I am always looking for other emerging leaders. I am looking for individuals sent to me by God who have displayed a willingness to serve in one capacity or another in our community. I am looking for people who possess influence assets. I firmly believe that people are our most appreciable asset, and when we invest in their hearts and lives, we have the potential for a great return on our investment.

The great industrialist, Andrew Carnegie, said, "Men are developed the same way gold is mined. When gold is mined, several tons of dirt must be moved to get an ounce of gold; but one doesn't go into the mine looking for dirt; one goes in looking for the gold." I agree wholeheartedly.

I am looking for the following personal attributes in emerging leaders:

1. I look for people with passionate enthusiasm, men and women of zeal. Enthusiasm is contagious.
2. I look for people of insight and wisdom.
3. I look for people with relational charisma, a pleasing and attractive personality.
4. I look for people who are productive by nature, because people are attracted to those who get things done and make things happen.
5. I look for people who have character, people of honor who know how to honor others in their life and have developed within themselves a basic honor code and are morally sound.

6. I look for people who are courageous and bold. Others will be attracted to those who, in an hour of crisis, know what to do and keep their head about them. They will become leaders like the sons of Issachar. In this hour of crisis, if we, as a church, can get a word from God—a strategy—we will be able to turn the nations to Him.

Identifying emerging leaders is only a first step. Working with them and developing them then requires much more time and patience. Our efforts must be spent in walking with, relating to and learning to trust these up-and-coming leaders. But identifying them and working to bring forth their gifts is the heart of God for the Church in this hour.

God is raising up a new breed of leaders. We must remember that they will not look like the average stereotypical leader of the past. And they will not, in the beginning stages, at least, look like a finished product. Keep in mind that these are diamonds in the rough. Treat them accordingly. Value them!

I feel certain that the Lord is much more interested in the fruit of the Spirit and the character and integrity of a leader than he is in our specific talents, skills, abilities and gifts. Remember, therefore, when you are looking for and selecting leaders to work in your particular aspect or area of ministry, that this is one of the important key functions of your leadership role.

When you select a leader to work with you, you are not just affecting that individual and their future. He or she will have a direct impact and influence on many other people, those whom they then lead. The result will be a long line of followers who will look, act, work and relate very much like this new leader relates to you. Let me give you some examples:

- If you are selecting a person who doesn't seem to think it's all that important to be punctual and always seems to be running late, the people that he or she influences or trains will likely have that same bad tendency.

- If the person you are working with happens to be a volunteer leader, one who views him- or herself as more of a volunteer than a leader (and, consequently, doesn't give their role the importance and urgency it deserves), thinking to themselves, "It's not important because I'm just a volunteer; they're not paying me to do this," their followers will develop that same attitude.

- If the leadership development you are undertaking is church related, and that person's concept of the church suffers from old wounds received in church in the past, before you release them into leadership, make sure they receive the healing they need. I have found that most of the leaders the Lord sends me (like myself), need some healing. Still, keep in mind that they are your best investment.

When our Lord Jesus began looking for the leaders He would train, He took time to pray about it. It is very important that, as we are selecting leaders or individuals who are looking for discipleship or mentoring, we make sure to seek and find the heart of God in this matter. If the individual I am considering is married or in some other form of committed covenant relationship, before I commit to the leadership training process, I must make sure that their partner, their pastor and/or spouse is supportive of this new venture. I certainly want to make sure that the individual him- or herself is willing to commit the necessary time to the process.

Obviously, I want to connect and relate properly and appropriately to each individual. I want to meet them where they are. I might use a scale of A, B and

C, A being a low level of involvement and commitment and C being a high level. If I meet someone who visits our church or fellowship, and I don't have very high expectations of them, my conversation with them will be on a lighter note. If I have high expectations of them, but they are not prepared to commit to that extent, I will be disappointed. By the same token, if someone is really locked into the vision and hope of the future we have on our hearts and lives and is ready to make a level-C commitment to our relationship, and I'm not sure of them, then they will be disappointed. We have to come to agreement.

One of the things that has caused some hurt, disappointment and frustration in my own life is having unrealistic expectations of someone that was put on them by others or even by me. I must be patient in pursuing a relationship, meeting each individual where they are. I must also be open minded and willing to change as that relationship matures.

Observation is key to identifying and relating to emerging leaders. It is simply an awareness factor. Observing and listening and, at times, looking beyond a person's words and actions, really trying to find their heart. This is essential.

Identifying and selecting leaders is so important because the success of a leader and an organization is highly dependent upon the quality of the leaders produced. Don't take this responsibility lightly.

Father, as we lead others, as we impart all that You have given us to those You bring into our path, may we have the spiritual insight to identify the emerging leaders You are raising up to usher in the greatest end-time event the world has ever known.

Lord, show us the gold in people. Teach us to invest our time and hearts, to help refine that gold by mentoring and discipling this new breed, which is part of the great end-time army.

Thank You, Lord, for giving us this privilege and entrusting emerging leaders to us, to speak and impart Your ways and Your will into their lives.

**In Jesus' name,
Amen!**

ANYONE CAN SHARE A THOUGHT AND MAKE A QUICK CONVERT, BUT MAKING DISCIPLES TAKES TIME, EFFORT, LOVE AND PATIENCE!

Chapter 3

What Is God Looking for in a Leader?

Psalm 24:3-4

> *Who may ascend the mountain of the* LORD?
>   *Who may stand in his holy place?*
> *The one who has clean hands and a pure heart,*
>   *who does not trust in an idol*
>   *or swear by a false god.*

There are fundamental basics that every leader should possess. Those aspiring to leadership, therefore, must grow in these basics and let these basics become foundational to their everyday life.

In order to lead, there is an equipping process. You cannot lead people to a place where you have not walked nor been equipped for during the seasons of your life. I can't dispute that a leader may be born in his mother's womb, but he or she is molded and made in the furnace of adversity, the furnace of affliction.

A leader must be a man or woman of the Word and of prayer, knowing that the Word is our final authority. A leader must show the fruit of the Word in their life. Like a tree with its roots going deep, their walk needs to reflect a grounding and a balance in the Spirit. I have always said: "Too much of the Word makes you dry up; too much of the Spirit makes you blow up. The Word and the Spirit together makes you grow up."

A leader needs to understand and discern spiritual authority and spiritual protocol, have a servant's heart and be hungry for the things of God.

God is raising up a generation unto holiness, and we, too, as leaders. must lead these new ones into holiness. The Word of God asks the questions, *"Who may ascend the mountain of the* LORD? *Who may stand in his holy place?"* and then it answers those questions: *"The one who has clean hands and a pure heart, who does not trust in an idol or swear by a false god."* These are God's requirements, and they should be ours too.

A leader must be conscious of the need for unity. The heartbeat of God is a church with covenantal relationships, where ministries, families and individuals are all flowing in corporate unity, to fulfill

God's plan and purpose for this season. Paul was clear in his letter to the Ephesians:

Ephesians 4:3

Make every effort to keep the unity of the Spirit through the bond of peace.

No leader can ignore the need for unity.

Giving is another strong aspect to look for in quality leadership. A leader understands the revelation of sowing into the Kingdom and the Kingdom principle of tithing. They understand the power and importance of tithing and giving. For men and women who have a heart for God, giving begins with their local body.

Now, let's concentrate on several important aspects of leadership, beginning with character.

CHARACTER

Character is the first thing I look for in a leader, and there are no short cuts to character. For many years I taught business, and was involved in buying, renovating and selling real estate. As the saying goes, when it comes to real estate, "The important thing is location, location and location."

With leadership for the Church, it is integrity, integrity and integrity.

Billy Graham was once asked about the three greatest areas that the church needs to work on. He answered, "Integrity, integrity and integrity." The definition of *integrity* is "the quality or state of being complete, sound, whole or in perfect condition." A synonym for *integrity* is "honesty," meaning "respectable, credible, commendable; one who will not lie, cheat or steal, one who is truthful, trustworthy, upright and free of deceit, genuine, pure, open honorable and reliable."

Che Ann, the great apostle, when speaking of character, said that many leaders are introduced as "Pastor So and So" or "Prophet So and So," who "pastors a thousand-member church" or "has a TV show," or "is the author of five books," or "someone who travels extensively," or "Our guest today has a Ph.D.," etc., etc. However, it is much more important to be known by our character traits. And could you imagine the impact if we were to be introduced solely that way?

We are undoubtedly in a season of sifting in the worldwide Church. It is essential that we allow the Holy Spirit to work into us the character traits and the heart of Christ Himself.

Each of us needs to preach the whole counsel of God. We need to be open to the restoration of the Church. We need to have an understanding of Church government and protocol. We certainly need to have hungry hearts and be seekers of God's face in this hour. And nothing is more important than allowing the work of the Spirit to be fulfilled in and through us. That is the hard work of the Holy Spirit in our daily lives. Can we commit ourselves to this process?

Even after basic training, in our walk of discipleship and seasons of practical training, where we earn our stripes concerning servanthood and relationship, are we willing to continue in a place of accountability with a teachable spirit? When we are green, it means that we are growing. When we are ripe, it means that we are nearly rotten. What am I trying to say? When we think we know everything, then we really don't know anything at all.

Can we finally, as a body, as a company of leaders, come to a place of real maturity and embrace real humility, so that the work of ministry that we are called to can stand the test of time, and we may bear fruit that lasts?

FAITH

Another essential element for a leader is faith. You simply cannot lead in the Kingdom of God without it. You can't even please God without it (see Hebrews 11:6). Here are five types of faith a leader must operate in:

1. The Gift of Faith

The gift of faith is the special ability that God gives to certain members of the Body of Christ to discern, with extraordinary confidence, His will and purposes for His work, and to act on His promises with confidence and unwavering belief in His ability to fulfill His purposes.

We see this in Paul's first letter to the Corinthians:

1 Corinthians 12:7-9, NKJV

But the manifestation of the Spirit is given to each one for the profit of all: for to one is given the word of wisdom through the Spirit, to another the word of knowledge through the same Spirit, to another faith by the same Spirit, to another gifts of healings by the same Spirit.

Jesus Himself taught:

Mark 11:22-23, NKJV

Have faith in God. For assuredly, I say to you, whoever says to this mountain, "Be removed and be cast into the sea," and does not doubt in his heart, but believes that those things he says will be done, he will have whatever he says.

The writer to the Hebrews declared:

Hebrews 11:1-2, NKJV

Now faith is the substance of things hoped for, the evidence of things not seen. For by it the elders obtained a good testimony.

People with this gift act with confidence and boldness in God's ability to overcome obstacles. They also have a boldness that rises up in situations that seem impossible. They not only believe that God *can* do something, but that He *will* do something. This is a supernatural knowing. I know that I know that God is about to do a miracle. This gift belongs to God and is given to us. Therefore no man can take credit for it.

2. The Fruit of Faith

The gift of faith is imparted from God, but the fruit of faith is produced by the Holy Spirit. The gift of faith can move mountains, but the fruit of faith is what is required for daily living:

Galatians 5:22-23, NKJV

> *But the fruit of the Spirit is love, joy, peace, longsuffering, kindness, goodness, faithfulness, gentleness, self-control. Against such there is no law.*

The fruit of faith enables us to walk and live by faith:

Romans 5:2, NKJV

> *Through whom also we have access by faith into this grace in which we stand, and rejoice in hope of the glory of God.*

The fullness of the fruit of the Spirit called faith depends upon us and how much we are willing to allow it to develop in our lives. There is a cost to developing spiritual growth. It means laying down your life, your personal wants and desires for God's will in your life. From the nurturing of spiritual growth comes a strong faith.

3. Faith to Live By

Habakkuk 2:4, NKJV
> *Behold the proud,*
> *His soul is not upright in him;*
> *But the just shall live by his faith.*

Hebrews 10:38, NKJV
> *Now the just shall live by faith,*
> *But if anyone draws back,*
> *My soul has no pleasure in him.*

Hebrews 11:1-2, NKJV
> *Now faith is the substance of things hoped for, the evidence of things not seen. For by it the elders obtained a good report.*

God wants us to trust in Him daily and not lean on our own understanding. This requires that we be in God's Word daily, meditating on His Word and being in prayer, letting all our requests be made known to Him:

Philippians 4:6

> *Do not be anxious about anything, but in every situation, by prayer and petition, with thanksgiving, present your requests to God.*

Faith is an action, and faith without action is dead. Active faith gives substance to what you hope to come to pass. Faith, therefore, is believing and acting upon the Word of God.

4. Enduring Faith

The definition of *endure* in the *Miriam Webster Dictionary* is as follows: "1: to undergo (as a hardship) especially without giving in: suffer <endured great pain> 2: to regard with acceptance or tolerance <could not endure noisy children> intransitive verb 3: to continue in the same state: last <the style endured for centuries> 4: to remain firm under suffering or misfortune without yielding <though it is difficult, we must endure>."

The Word of God tells us:

James 1:3-4

> *Because you know that the testing of your faith produces perseverance. Let perseverance finish*

its work so that you may be mature and complete, not lacking anything.

James 1:12

Blessed is the one who perseveres under trial because, having stood the test, that person will receive the crown of life that the Lord has promised to those who love him.

Romans 1:17

For in the gospel the righteousness of God is revealed—a righteousness that is by faith from first to last, just as it is written: "The righteous will live by faith."

We need faith that endures hardship. Enduring faith means that you are passing the test and entering into the promise. The fact that there is a test just means that a promotion is coming. The promise of Abraham came only after many wilderness testings, and this is God's model for us—individually and corporately.

Some great examples of enduring faith are:

Noah: While there had never been any rain before, Noah had faith to build an ark, and it took him a hundred and twenty years. In the midst of mocking, he continued to hear God's voice and built an ark to the exact measurements God had given him.

Esther: She risked her life to come before the king without a previous invitation. Her words of faith were: *"If I am to die, then die I will"* (Esther 4:16, CEB). She had faith to endure so that she could see her people saved from the extermination planned for them by the wicked Haman.

Daniel: His enduring faith was a model of faithfulness, as he and his three friends persisted in their faith despite the threats issued by several foreign rulers whom they served with dedication. They encouraged faithful persistence while facing persecution.

Jesus: He, of course, is the greatest role model of all. His enduring faith kept Him to the point of allowing Himself to be nailed to a cross and go through a gruesome death, knowing the joy that was set before him.

Hebrews 12:1-2

Therefore, since we are surrounded by such a great cloud of witnesses, let us throw off everything that hinders and the sin that so easily entangles. And let us run with perseverance the race marked out for us, fixing our eyes on Jesus, the pioneer and perfecter of faith. For the joy set before him he endured the cross, scorning its shame, and sat down at the right hand of the throne of God.

Paul: His life is an excellent example of how faith in God can help a believer endure hardship. He wrote:

2 Corinthians 11:23-27

I have worked much harder, been in prison more frequently, been flogged more severely, and been exposed to death again and again. Five times I received from the Jews the forty lashes minus one. Three times I was beaten with rods, once I was stoned, three times I was shipwrecked. I spent a night and a day in the open sea, and I have been constantly on the move. I have been in danger from rivers, in danger from bandits, in danger from my own countrymen, in danger from Gentiles; in danger in the city, in danger in the country, in danger at sea; and in danger from false brothers. I have labored and toiled and have often gone without sleep; I have known hunger and thirst and have often gone without food; I have been cold and naked.

As Paul went through these various trials, he did not lose sight of his victory. He even encouraged others:

2 Corinthians 4:8-9

We are hard pressed on every side, but not crushed; perplexed, but not in despair; persecuted, but not abandoned; struck down, but not destroyed.

Even though Paul experienced a great deal of hardship, his enduring faith enabled him to remain confident in God through every trial, and that is an example for us.

5. Faithfulness

Faithfulness is making life's choices based on our faith. The righteous shall live by faith: it is a characteristic of one who is reliable and dependable, someone you can count on.

God is always faithful:

Psalm 33:4

> *For the word of the LORD is right and true;*
> *he is faithful in all he does.*

2 Timothy 2:13

> *If we are faithless,*
> *he remains faithful,*
> *for he cannot disown himself.*

True leadership is service in faithfulness. God's way is very different than the world's. He is much more interested in the fruit of the Spirit and the character than He is our gifts. One sure mechanism He puts into place for promotion is faithfulness. He appreciates faithfulness because it is part of His character. He is the one whose name is Faithfulness and Truth (see Isaiah 25:1, KJV). But it's not just His name; it's a revelation of His nature, meaning that God is absolutely trustworthy. He is not a man that He should lie (see Numbers 23:19). He is the same yesterday, today and forever (see Hebrews 13:8), so His nature never changes. Throughout the Scriptures, His faithfulness is revealed:

Deuteronomy 7:9

He is the faithful God.

1 Thessalonians 5:24

The one who calls you is faithful.

2 Thessalonians 3:3

The Lord is faithful.

Hebrews 10:23

He who promised is faithful.

Our faithful God is looking for men and women who are also faithful. In the Hebrew, the word for *faithfulness* is derived from the same root as trust, loyalty, and steadfastness. Our God appreciates, honors and celebrates faithfulness.

I am looking forward (and you probably are as well) to that moment in time when I will hear the Lord speak the words, "Good and faithful servant." "Good servant" would not be enough on that day. I want to hear the words *"Well done, good and faithful servant"* (Matthew 25:23).

Here are some examples of men of the Bible who were faithful:

What Is God Looking for in a Leader?

1. Moses was faithful (see Numbers 12:7 and Hebrews 3:5).
2. Hezekiah was faithful (see 2 Chronicles 31:20).
3. Paul was faithful (see 1 Timothy 1:12, KJV).
4. David was faithful (see 1 Kings 3:6, AMPC).
5. The saints at Ephesus were faithful (see Ephesians 1:1).
6. Tychicus was declared faithful twice (see Ephesians 6:21 and Colossians 4:7).
7. The brothers of Colosse were faithful (see Colossians 1:2).
8. Epaphras was faithful (see Colossians 1:7).
9. Onesimus was faithful (see Colossians 4:9).
10. Silvanus was faithful (see 1 Peter 5:12).
11. Antipas was faithful unto death (see Revelation 2:13).

God valued each of these people for their faithfulness. Have you ever heard of Epaphras? What about Tychicus? The interesting thing about these men is that the Bible does not tell us how many people were in their congregations, or how big their ministries were. Today, ministers are often judged by these standards, but all we know about these men of the Bible is that they were faithful. With God, that was enough.

Very few people achieve greatness overnight. God's Word declares:

Zechariah 4:10, TLV

For who despises the day of small things?

Job 8:7, NLT

And though you started with little,
you will end with much.

The New International Version of the Bible renders that verse this way:

Your beginnings will seem humble,
so prosperous will your future be.

Consider, if you will, these facts:

- Moses was a stutterer who became a deliver.
- Gideon was a farmer who became a general.
- Deborah was a housewife who became a judge.
- David was a shepherd who became a king.
- Elisha was a servant who became a prophet.
- Esther was an orphan who became a queen.
- Peter was a fisherman who became an apostle.

What Is God Looking for in a Leader?

If you are faithful in the little things, God has promised to give you more (see Luke 16:10-12). Whether it is in your marital relationship, ministry or business, you will find one of the keys to lasting success is faithfulness. God is looking for leaders who are faithful.

The world puts a great premium on talent and ability, but God understands the makings of a leader, character and loyalty. Faithfulness is the key to lasting success in His Kingdom.

Many times the initial success of a leader is short circuited by a lack of faithfulness. Ability may determine what you get, but faithfulness will determine what you keep. Faithfulness will keep you where your talent brings you.

When people evaluate a man or woman's lifetime accomplishments, they normally don't remember how fast they got to the top, but rather how long they stayed there. Success or failure in the life of a leader usually occurs one day at a time.

Here are nine biblical rewards for faithfulness:

1. Faithfulness attracts God's attention. *"My eyes will be on the faithful in the land, that they may dwell with me"* (Psalm 101:6).
2. Faithfulness releases God's blessings. *"A faithful man will be richly blessed"* (Proverbs 28:20).

3. Faithfulness gives God the opportunity to prove Himself to you. The Psalmist wrote about God, *"To the faithful you show yourself faithful"* (Psalm 18:25).
4. Faithfulness produces safety and security. *"The Lord preserves the faithful"* (Psalm 31:23, NKJV).
5. Faithfulness releases reward. *"The Lord rewards every man for his ... faithfulness"* (1 Samuel 26:23, ESV).
6. Faithfulness in small things leads to big things. *"You have been faithful with a few things; I will put you in charge of many things"* (Matthew 25:21).
7. Faithfulness protects you from accusations of wrongdoing. No fault or wrong could be found in Daniel because he was a faithful servant (see Daniel 6:4).
8. Faithfulness is valuable because of its rarity. *"Most men will proclaim every one his own goodness; but a faithful man who can find?"* (Proverbs 20:6, KJ21).

Being faithful is not just for one area of your life. A faithful person is faithful in every area because faithfulness becomes an integral part of their character.

Father, I pray for all who read this, that right now, as a body, as a company of leaders, we come to a place of real maturity and embrace real humility, so that the work of ministry that we are called to can stand the test of time, and we may bear fruit that lasts.

I pray, Lord, that we would understand the many facets of faith. Like those who have gone before us, the trail blazers who have endured, persevered and overcome, plowing and advancing Your Kingdom, that we also would be known as men and women of Faith.

In Jesus' name!
Amen!

AFTER ONE OF OUR REVIVAL MEETINGS, I WAS THANKING THE LORD FOR THE GREAT SERVICES. HE SPOKE TO MY HEART QUIETLY AND SAID,

"IT'S NOT ABOUT GREAT MEETINGS; IT'S ABOUT RAISING UP SONS AND DAUGHTERS"!

Chapter 4

Developing Honor, Integrity and Character

Romans 1:1

> *Paul, a servant of Christ Jesus, called to be an apostle and set apart for the gospel of God.*

How could I write a book on leadership and not emphasize honor, integrity and character? This is especially true when it comes to spiritual leadership.

Jesus was, by far, the best CEO model in the Bible, and the book of Proverbs can supply you with all the wisdom, principles, foundation and motivation necessary to establish yourself in any field of endeavor, whether in business, government or ministry, and, of course, in your family relationships.

The Bible is the blueprint for successful Christian living. One of the first things you need to do as you commit yourself to the call and life of leadership, is to establish for yourself a personal moral code. I'm not talking here about a religious formula. I'm talking about a code of morals and ethics that you personally establish for yourself and for the way you will handle all of your affairs. Draw a line in the sand for yourself.

I would imagine that all of us, at one time or another in our lives and careers, have tried to take the easy way out, some short cut, maybe some pie-in-the-sky or get-rich-quick scheme and, somewhere along the way, have crossed that line or even compromised our integrity. Maybe it was for that pot of gold that is at the end of the rainbow. Maybe it was out of fear and not wanting to confront an individual or situation.

Most men, like all rivers, seem to take the path of least resistance, only to learn that there is no such thing as a free lunch and that, with every choice and every decision, there is a consequence. It's scientific and it's spiritual: whatever a man sows, that's what he will reap (see Galatians 6:7-8).

As we begin to step into any leadership role, the most important thing we need to do is to protect ourselves from ourselves. We do that by establishing accountability partners. The Bible says:

Proverbs 27:17

> *As iron sharpens iron,*
> *so one person sharpens another.*

Proverbs 17:17

> *A friend loves at all times,*
> *and a brother is born for a time of adversity.*

I need a brother or brothers to stand with me in the place of relationship and accountability, someone who is not afraid to hold my feet to the fire, someone who is willing to risk our relationship for my good, someone who cares enough about me to speak the truth in love (see Ephesians 4:15).

Certainly, a spouse is an important part of that network of protection, but that is not enough in and of itself. My wife, Mave, is a wonderful woman of God, a great partner and friend, lover and soulmate, but I also need to surround myself with others. She is strong and honest, but our relationship is multi-faceted and can sometimes complicate the process.

I remember once, early in our marriage, mentioning to the Lord that WOW! He had given me Mave, and she was a strong partner and, surely, no pushover. Then the Lord said to me, "You're pretty strong yourself, and if I had given you a pushover, you probably would have pushed her over." Isn't it good that the Lord knows us? What's even better is that He still loves us, even though He knows us.

I'm believing that God will send some accountability partners your way. That support system and network is necessary for your success. I have my wife, my leadership team and my board of directors as a core group of people the Lord has put around me to provoke me to holiness and challenge me to good works.

Now, let's talk about developing honor, integrity and character.

HONOR

What is it?

- Personal integrity; allegiance to moral principles
- (a.) Fame or glory (b.) a person or thing that wins this for another: he is an honor to the school (often plural) great respect, regard, esteem, etc. or an outward sign of this
- High or noble rank (often plural)
- To do honor to (a.) to pay homage to (b.) to be a credit to

- Do the honors (a.) to serve as a host or hostess (b.) to perform a social act, such as carving meat, proposing a toast, etc.
- In honor bound under a moral obligation
- In honor of out of respect for
- On one's honor, upon one's honor, on the pledge of one's word or good name
- The concept of a direct relation between one's virtues (or "values") and their status within society.

WHAT DOES IT MEAN TO BE HONOR-BOUND?

Romans 1:1, KJV

Paul, a bondservant of Jesus Christ, called to be an apostle, separated to the gospel of God.

"Bound by or placed under the obligation of honor." *Honor* may be defined as "the deferential recognition by word or sign of another's worth or station." I show honor to another by giving him his title (if he has one), by raising my hat to him, or by yielding to him a place of precedence. In this way, I express my sense of his worth, and, at the same time, profess my inferiority to him.

Among the goods that are external to man, honor holds the first place, above wealth and power. It is that which we especially give to God. It is the highest reward which we can bestow on virtue, and it is what men naturally prize the most. The apostle Paul bid us to give honor to whom honor is due:

Romans 13:7, KJV

> *Render therefore to all their dues: tribute to whom tribute is due; custom to whom custom; fear to whom fear; honour to whom honour.*

To withhold honor when it is due or to dishonor someone is a sin against justice and entails the obligation of making suitable restitution.

Honor is also a social term describing how people within a society evaluate one another. Most occurrences of honor in the Old Testament are translations of some form of *kabod,* while in the New Testament they are derivatives of *timao.* These terms are generally used with reference to the honor granted fellow human beings, though in some cases they are used to describe the honor a person grants God.

The root of *kabod* literally means "heavy or weighty." The figurative meaning, however, is far more common: "to give weight to someone." To honor someone, then, is it to give weight or to grant a person a position of respect and even authority in one's life.

A person grants honor most frequently on the basis of position, status, or wealth, but it can and should also be granted on the basis of character.

While honor is an internal attitude of respect, courtesy and reverence, it should be accompanied by appropriate attention or even obedience. Honor without such action is incomplete; it is a flippant service. God said of the Israelites:

Isaiah 29:13

> *These people come near to me with their mouth*
> *and honor me with their lips,*
> *but their hearts are far from me.*

God was saying that their worship of Him was based on human rules they have been taught. God is honored when we praise Him sincerely, but He is also honored when we obey Him out of a sincere heart:

1 Corinthians 6:20

> *You were bought at a price. Therefore honor God*
> *with your bodies.*

In the same way, parents are honored through the obedience of their children.

The source of all honor is God, on the basis of His position as sovereign Creator and of His character as a loving Father. God the Father has bestowed honor on His Son, Jesus Christ:

John 5:23

> *That all may honor the Son just as they honor the Father. Whoever does not honor the Son does not honor the Father, who sent him.*

God bestowed honor on humanity by creating man a little lower than the angels.

Psalm 8:5-6

> *You have made them a little lower than the angels and crowned them with glory and honor. You made them rulers over the works of your hands; you put everything under their feet.*

God also created spheres of authority within human government, the church and the home. The positions of authority in those spheres are to receive honor implicitly. Granting honor to others is an essential experience in the believer's life. Christians are to bestow honor on those to whom honor is due. The believer is to honor God, for He is the sovereign

Head of the Universe and His character is unsurpassed. The believer is to honor those in positions of earthly authority, such as governing authorities, as Paul taught in Romans 13:1-7.

Even slaves were to honor their masters:

1 Timothy 6:1

> *All who are under the yoke of slavery should consider their masters worthy of full respect, so that God's name and our teaching may not be slandered.*

As noted, children are to honor their parents:

Exodus 20:12

> *Honor your father and your mother, so that you may live long in the land the LORD your God is giving you.*

As a participant in the Church, the believer is also called to honor Jesus Christ, the Head of the Church:

John 5:23

> *That all may honor the Son just as they honor the Father. Whoever does not honor the Son does not honor the Father, who sent him.*

Every believer is called to honor fellow believers:

Romans 12:10

> *Be devoted to one another in love. Honor one another above yourselves.*

Believers are also called to honor widows:

1 Timothy 5:3

> *Give proper recognition to those widows who are really in need.*

While the reception of honor is a positive experience, it is not to be sought:

Luke 14:7-8

> *When he noticed how the guests picked the places of honor at the table, he told them this parable: "When someone invites you to a wedding feast, do not take the place of honor, for a person more distinguished than you may have been invited."*

When honor comes from others by reason of position or status, it is not to be taken for granted. The recipients should seek to merit the honor given through godly living. Honor can be lost through disobedience or disrepute.

It should be noted that, in exceptional cases, dishonor can be a mark of discipleship. This refers, of course, to the honor (or dishonor, in this case) of the world:

2 Corinthians 6:8

Through glory and dishonor, bad report and good report; genuine, yet regarded as impostors.

INTEGRITY

What is it? Integrity is "a concept of consistency of actions, values, methods, measures, principles, expectations and outcomes." In ethics, integrity is regarded as "the honesty and truthfulness or accuracy of one's actions." Integrity can be regarded as the opposite of hypocrisy, in that it regards internal consistency as a virtue and suggests that parties holding apparently-conflicting values should account for the discrepancy or alter their beliefs.

Our word *integrity* stems from the Latin adjective *integer,* meaning "whole or complete." In this context, integrity is "the inner sense of wholeness deriving from qualities such as honesty and consistency of

70

character." As such, one may judge that others "have integrity" to the extent that they act according to the values, beliefs and principles they claim to hold.

Some more definitions of integrity:

1. Firm adherence to a code of especially moral or artistic values: incorruptibility
2. An unimpaired condition: soundness
3. The quality or state of being complete or undivided: completeness

One of the important elements of integrity is consistency. If we are unpredictable, if our decisions are dependent upon the day of the week and the way we are feeling at the moment, others are unlikely to see us as maintaining integrity.

Read through Daniel chapters 1 to 3. There we see Daniel and his friends sticking with their principles, despite pressure to the contrary. This is a theme which reoccurs throughout the book of Daniel. You, too, can and should walk in integrity.

Establishing Principles

When confronted with a challenging situation, the first step is to determine what our principles are. This may not be as easy as it sounds, particularly when faced with a difficult decision. To work through this study, you will need to use an example which you are either faced with currently (preferably) or have experienced recently.

What are your principles that apply to this situation? Write them down. This is very important. While we think that we know what our principles are, setting them down on paper is a real test of whether that clarity is genuine. Don't be surprised if you find this to be difficult. Most people need some quality thinking time to arrive at clarity concerning their principles.

Joseph had principles that guided his actions in a moment of crisis:

Genesis 39:6-9

So Potiphar left everything he had in Joseph's care; with Joseph in charge, he did not concern himself with anything except the food he ate. Now Joseph was well-built and handsome, and after a while his master's wife took notice of Joseph and said, "Come to bed with me!"
But he refused. "With me in charge," he told her, "my master does not concern himself with anything in the house; everything he owns he

has entrusted to my care. No one is greater in this house than I am. My master has withheld nothing from me except you, because you are his wife. How then could I do such a wicked thing and sin against God?"

Here we see the honor, integrity and character of Joseph in a difficult situation. Potiphar was a eunuch. Pharaoh demanded this of his closest advisors to prevent them from rising up against him. Mrs. Potiphar had married him, probably for position and prominence, but their relationship was not a happy one nor a normal one. Probably affairs were allowed her, as long as she kept it "hush, hush" and didn't humiliate her husband. Joseph could not accept this.

As noted earlier, Daniel was another principled person:

Daniel 6:1-5

It pleased Darius to appoint 120 satraps to rule throughout the kingdom, with three administrators over them, one of whom was Daniel. The satraps were made accountable to them so that the king might not suffer loss. Now Daniel so distinguished himself among the administrators and the satraps by his exceptional qualities that the king planned to set him over the whole kingdom. At this, the administrators and the satraps tried to find grounds for charges against Daniel in his conduct of government affairs, but they were unable to do so. They could find no corruption in him, because he was trustworthy and neither corrupt nor negligent. Finally these men said, "We will never find any basis for charges against this man Daniel unless it has something to do with the law of his God."

As with Joseph, Daniel was consistent in his honesty and character, and his enemies could find nothing against him.

Jesus said he could not find any deceit in Nathaniel, brother of Philip, His disciple:

John 1:44-47

Philip, like Andrew and Peter, was from the town of Bethsaida. Philip found Nathanael and told him, "We have found the one Moses wrote about in the Law, and about whom the prophets also wrote—Jesus of Nazareth, the son of Joseph."
"Nazareth! Can anything good come from there?" Nathanael asked.
"Come and see," said Philip.

When Jesus saw Nathanael approaching, he said of him, "Here truly is an Israelite in whom there is no deceit."

To find a man, living in the midst of so much corruption, walking in uprightness before his Maker, was a subject worthy of the attention of God Himself. Our Lord commended Nathanael for his integrity.

What does integrity do for you?

1 Kings 9:4-5, NKJV

Now if you walk before Me as your father David walked, in integrity of heart and in uprightness, to do according to all that I have commanded you, and if you keep My statutes and My judgments, then I will establish the throne of your kingdom over Israel forever, as I promised David your father, saying, "You shall not fail to have a man on the throne of Israel."

Throne = authority. Integrity establishes and reserves for you a place of authority. God promised the line of David perpetual authority, as long as they walked in integrity before Him.

Job was another Bible character whose integrity was tested:

Job 2:3

> *Then the LORD said to Satan, "Have you con-*
> *sidered my servant Job, that there is none like*
> *him on the earth, a blameless and upright man,*
> *one who fears God and shuns evil? And still he*
> *holds fast to his integrity, although you incited*
> *me against him, to destroy him without any*
> *reason."*

Hold on to your integrity in any trial. Character is not made under pressure; it is revealed under pressure. God stood up and took notice of Job because he did not make excuses. Instead, he held fast to his integrity:

Job 27:1-5, NKJV

> *Moreover Job continued his discourse, and said:*
>
> *"As God lives, who has taken away my justice,*
> *And the Almighty, who has made my soul bitter,*
> *As long as my breath is in me,*
> *And the breath of God in my nostrils,*
> *My lips will not speak wickedness,*

Nor my tongue utter deceit.
Far be it from me
That I should say you are right;
Till I die I will not put away my integrity from me.'

As you can see, Job was determined to hold fast to his integrity until the end—at all costs. He had perseverance. The Bible says that the righteous will persevere until the end:

What all will integrity do for you?

- Your integrity will preserve (defend, sustain, uphold) you. *"Let integrity and uprightness preserve me, for I wait for you"* (Psalm 25:21, NKJV).
- Your integrity will vindicate you (as in a court of law). You shall not slip. *"Vindicate me, O Lord, for I have walked in my integrity. I have also trusted in the Lord; I shall not slip"* (Psalm 26:1, NKJV).
- God will redeem you and be merciful to you because of your integrity. *"But as for me, I will walk in my integrity; redeem me and be merciful to me"* (Psalm 26:11, NKJV).
- Integrity preserves you, and because of it God will sustain you! He will give you strength. *"As for me, You uphold me in my integrity, and set me before your face forever"* (Psalm 41:12, NKJV).

- Integrity will keep you in righteous paths for His name's sake. The Lord will ordain your steps. *"He who walks with integrity walks securely, but he who perverts his ways will become known"* (Proverbs 10:9, NKJV).

- Integrity will guide or pilot you. You will be on auto-pilot as the Holy Spirit leads you into all truth. *"The integrity of the upright will guide them, but the perversity of the unfaithful will destroy them"* (Proverbs 11:3, NKJV).

- Your children will be blessed by God because of your integrity, a legacy left behind. *"The righteous man walks in his Integrity, his children are blessed after him"* (Proverbs 20:7, NKJV).

- As a mentor, your disciples will be exhorted and instructed by your integrity. As a Christian, people are watching you. As a man or woman of God, you are under a microscope. *"Likewise, exhort the young men to be sober-minded, in all things showing yourself to be a pattern of good works; in doctrine showing integrity, reverence, incorruptibility"* (Titus 2:6-7, NKJV).

In the final analysis, integrity is this: You do what is right, just because it is right.

CHARACTER

The true measure of your real character is what you would do if you knew you would never be caught or found out. Formed in the small matters of life by the things that really matter, integrity of character is the foundation over which everything else in your life is built. Cheating on integrity or character creates cracks in your foundation. The more you cheat, the easier it becomes to do it ... until you become incapable of acting with integrity. Sooner or later your foundation will crack and everything will come tumbling down. Again, character is not created in crisis; a crisis only serves to reveal your true nature.

Honor, integrity and character ... these are not for sale. Ethical principles are not flexible. President Dwight D. Eisenhower said: "In order to be a leader, a man must have followers. And to have followers, a man must have their confidence. Hence, the supreme quality for a leader is, unquestionably, integrity. It allows others to trust you."

Others will come to trust in you only when you demonstrate a solid and firm character at all times. In other words, people will trust you because of your integrity. You begin to reach others when you begin to win their trust. When others begin to trust you, your level of influence will increase. Trust and respect are not bestowed; they are earned.

> **My prayer for you today is that the Lord would mold you and make you into the leader that He ordained you to be. He knew you would be here, even from the womb. May the love of God manifest in the midst of the Refiner's fire, in which He may burn away any and everything in your life that is not of Him. May He produce anew the gold and silver for the fulfillment of your destiny, so that the whole world can marvel at the work of His hands.**
>
> **In Jesus' name,**
> **Amen!**

YOU NEED TO MAKE SURE YOU ARE FOLLOWING SOMEONE WHO'S GOING WHERE YOU'RE GOING, OR YOU'LL END UP SOMEPLACE YOU'RE NOT SUPPOSED TO BE!

Chapter 5

Five Types of leaders

Ephesians 4:11-12

> *So Christ himself gave the apostles, the prophets, the evangelists, the pastors and teachers, to equip his people for works of service, so that the body of Christ may be built up.*

As leaders, we need to see ourselves more clearly and then see how we can change what we are doing to make it better. To walk in successful Christian leadership requires continual change on our part. It is the continual making and molding of who we are, how we lead, and how to alter our path when we must. In the process, everything is moving and changing; nothing remains the same.

Change is constant. Jesus is about changing and transforming us, transitioning us and transforming our hearts continually. We must get to a place in our own hearts where we honestly view ourselves, our heart and our ways. Then we will allow the changes to improve us as we continue our walk of faith.

Among the five-fold gifts, the pastor's job is the most difficult. We must honor the pastors who walk with us through the tough personal moments of life. We lift up TV ministries, multi-media outreach and itinerant ministers who come in and then leave. But they can't be your pastor. The one who walks with you through difficult times is your pastor.

Times have changed, and there are certain situations that we also need to adapt to, yet still maintain a viable spiritual influence. However, as the world changes and times change, we need to change with some of these things and become spiritually relevant to our current culture.

What we desperately need today are mentor leaders. Elijah was a mentor leader. He raised up a company of prophets, and one of those he raised up was Elisha, who became his successor.

Paul was a mentor leader, and he had the right concept of ministry. Ministry and leadership are all about relationship. Paul was covered by a council, and he answered to that council. When they disagreed, he went back and dealt with the issue.

Paul had his peers walking in right relationship with him. He was in right relationship with Barnabas, Peter, Timothy and Titus.

Jesus was a tremendous example of a mentoring leader. He lived with the disciples. They walked and talked together, and He had a different relationship with them than with the multitudes who followed Him. We will also have different relationship with different members of our church.

Jesus had one relationship with the multitudes and a very different relationship with the seventy-two who were around him. He had a more intimate relationship with the twelve and even a more intimate relationship with the three who went up with Him on the Mount of Transfiguration.

An example of the closeness Jesus had with John, who was called "the beloved disciple," came when Jesus was on the cross. He now turned over to John the role of caring for His own mother:

John 19:26-27

> *When Jesus saw his mother there, and the disciple whom he loved standing nearby, he said to her, "Woman, here is your son," and to the disciple, "Here is your mother." From that time on, this disciple took her into his home.*

84

Five Types of leaders

Jesus had a natural side of His life, and the people had difficulty at times differentiating the various sides of who He was. He had taken on the nature of man, but He was a mentor type of leader. He saw His disciples regularly, did things with them and took some of them with Him when He went to do some special miracle. The disciples not only witnessed Him feeding people on the mountainside, but He also gave them some of the food to distribute. He first demonstrated how to do it, doing it in front of them. Then He did it with them. Then, they did it.

The twelve disciples Jesus had an intimate relationship with gathered around Him at special times, and He took the parables apart and taught deeper truths to them than He did to the multitudes. They needed to know more than the average person, for they were to share their knowledge with many others. In this way, Jesus was multiplying Himself. These men were to do the same things He had done, and, in the process, raise up and train others to take their place. Jesus modeled this same method, as did Elijah and Paul.

I have found that there are basically five types of leaders. We may see ourselves in a few of these different positions and hopefully can eventually get back to where we know we should be. Let's now take a look at these five types of leaders.

1. POSITIONAL LEADERSHIP

In positional leadership, it is important to know who you are working with and the style they use. You need to know how to be a good follower and to work rightly in that particular environment. The following points are characteristics of positional leadership:

- I am the pastor, and so I am the boss. You don't have to respect me as a person, but you must respect my position.
- I am the boss, so you'll do it my way. It's my way or the highway.
- Do as I say, not as I do.
- There is little relationship between these leaders and those they lead.
- This is an impersonal way of ministry.
- These leaders might be strong and effective, but they will rarely touch you. They will teach you but not touch you.
- These leaders have strong authority, but they operate out of insecurity. They can't seem to connect personally.

2. DIRECTIONAL LEADERSHIP

Every form of leadership should be delegation-oriented. The more people you have the more delegating you will need to do. As leaders, we need to delegate and operate in this fully without exception. You can appoint, give direction and then bring correction. You give another person a responsibility, but you make sure you are able to go back later and bring any needed correction without damaging the relationship.

Directional leadership, however, is task oriented and it's all black and white. I agree that we must be black and white on holiness and integrity and our daily walk when developing leaders. But there is a limit. You have to remember that you are dealing with real people, people who deal every single day with real issues in their own lives. So, relationship has to be part of the mix. You cannot be black and white, cut and dried, on every point.

There has to be some leeway as you work with people who are going through things at the same time. This is why directional leadership can be too black and white. You either did it right or wrong;

there is no middle ground. This form of leadership lacks the personal touch and is more about a to-do list than it is about serving God.

3. Situational Leadership

The lines drawn in these last two forms of leadership have, to some degree, some specific boundaries or guidelines. You know where the line is drawn and what the boundaries are. With situational leadership, you are in the opposite ditch. My wife, Mave, always says, "For every mile of road, there are two miles of ditch, one on each side." With situational leadership:

- You decide what to do as you go along.
- The boundaries are obscure.
- You don't know how far you can go, what you can do or what you can't do.
- You are uncertain where the limit is, where the line is or what authority you have.
- Leadership, therefore, changes with every situation.
- Leadership is completely crisis driven. You handle the situations of the moment and adjust your decisions to meet every new situation.

- You go from one emergency crisis to another, and every decision is based on the situation, so there is line of demarcation.

The person working for a situational leader is like a child who has no parent to set sure lines and boundaries around him. God's commandments are not hard to follow when you understand the heart of a leader. God put barriers up around us for the same reason. We put up fences in our yards, not because we don't want our children to go out and play, but so that they will be safe when they do.

When working for situational leaders, you wonder where the fence is, or if there even is a fence. Your leaders make up the rules as they go, and each decision is made on the day it is needed. This type of leadership lacks foresight. There is a vision, but it is obscure. The vision holder has vision in their heart, but they have trouble casting the vision.

Casting the vision motivates me. to keep me in line with the vision, so I don't walk without constraint. If you don't tell the whole congregation, tell those who walk closely with you what the vision is and what the boundaries are. Better yet, prepare a job description, showing what authority and responsibility that person has been given. This rarely happens with situational leaders.

Let a person know what they have to do and what power and authority they have to do it. Understand that there is sovereign authority (God-given) and also delegated authority. When you delegate a function to me, I have to know, as a follower, that I have that delegated authority. I need to understand that I am supporting the vision of the leader. When a situation is encountered, I then do as my leader would do.

For example, when I worked for Pastor Wetzel, I knew his vision and in every situation I represented him. The same thing was true when I worked with Ruth Heflin. My authority was delegated to me by her or someone close to her. They, however, had sovereign authority.

4. MOM AND POP LEADERSHIP

This type of leadership is common in small settings where there are twenty to thirty people. Mom and Pop take all the credit and glory, but they also do all the work. A mega-ministry could never run this way.

The hardest thing for some people to do is to get that first potential leader and begin to delegate responsibility to them and to work with them to carry out effectively that assigned work. But you have to start somewhere. Pick someone, and then start bringing them close to you. Teach them what is needed, and then assign them a work to do.

Those who do the bulk of work in the majority of our churches are volunteers, not paid employees. They need to be led (which was the style of Jesus), and not bossed around. They may resent being bossed. Just as the Lord leads us, we must lead others.

Under Mom-and-Pop leadership, the few who do all the work are worn out and have no time to do many other important things because they are doing everything else. Worst of all, in that setting, other members get no opportunity to demonstrate their gifts or to grow in them. Therefore, no one gets praise or recognition except Mom and Pop, and the vision is not carried on or extended.

Ministry is not about money, so that fact that volunteers are not paid is not the problem. The problem is that they need the recognition of their gifts and the reward they receive from exercising them. If there is no opportunity for them, eventually they just might go elsewhere. At the very least, they are robbed of spiritual growth, and the vision suffers. It is vitally important to discover, put to work and recognize all the gifts in your house.

A helper can only be responsible for the revelation God has given them. When they walk in delegated authority, however, they take the vision that God gave the leader and conform to it. They are not, however, ultimately responsible for the fulfillment of that vision. Their leader is, because it came to them from the Lord. Helpers are responsible to honor leadership and the vision God put in their life.

5. Mentoring Leaders

The concepts of mentoring leadership will work in small settings or large. This always works under any circumstance. This style of leadership can be summarized as follows: I am in a particular place for a limited season. Let's say that I am there to pastor. But I am not the only minister there; we are all ministers together. If someone joins me in the work, they become part of the family, and as members of the family, we all have chores to do, and we all pull our weight.

Recognize that there are things other people can do that you, as a leader, are now doing. For example, greeters are very important at any church. They shake people's hands before and after the service, engaging them and forming relationships with them, asking them if they enjoyed the service and if they have any special needs. The person or persons you put on the door has to have the right personality and skills for this work. They should have the gift of hospitality and make everyone feel welcome and at home.

When first setting up protocol, find someone who is very responsible and trustworthy, develop a relationship with them and delegate the responsibility of opening and closing the church to them. Once you have developed a team and get them in place—the pastor, pastoral team, elders and deacons, etc.—then you don't need to go early every time. They now have that role and responsibility.

My goal is to build my way out of any work. A real leader is always developing a new leader to take over, so that if they are called away from the work for a season, the work will continue to run smoothly in their absence. And, if they are called to another work, this one will not collapse.

Take notice of your people. Is there someone always lingering at the end of every service? Pay attention to who is there at the end. Then assign them related duties.

The same goes for the job of catching people when they fall. Teach your people how to catch and then teach them how to teach other catchers and, finally, release them into a place of responsibility.

Assume, when you are called to build a church, that God will build it for you. Then work yourself out of every job. If I can do that job, then someone else can do it too. If I insist on always doing it, that other person will never be trained. If I give them an opportunity, they will grow in their gifts and abilities.

Therefore, when you build leaders, let them first see what you're doing and how you are doing it, so that they will know what *they* are to do. Then release them to do it.

When teaching others to counsel, for example, have them sit through counseling sessions with you while you counsel someone else, and, in this way, they will learn how to counsel.

From the beginning of any new work, I am always planning to pass the baton to someone else. So I start from the beginning deciding how that baton should be passed. I want to leave a legacy, a lasting work.

I don't like it when people do everything themselves. My leaders are to build other leaders. I am convinced that as long as I am building leaders, God will send me work. They won't replace me. I will be moving on up to other levels of authority.

Mentoring leadership gives others responsibility, but in Mom-and-Pop situations, there is little responsibility, authority, praise and/or recognition to spread around. As an example of delegating: at our campground in Canada, I have delegated authority for rental accommodations, grounds-keeping, sound and media, set-up, take-down, maintenance, etc., and so I know that each job will get done. Everyone who participates is recognized for the work they do. We need to love people enough to recognize their gifts and then give them jobs to do, so that they can develop their talents.

Wherever there is mom-and-pop leadership, there is short-sightedness. There is no long-term vision, and people cannot capture the existing vision because they are in sitting mode, not in participating mode. But church was not meant to be a spectator sport. It should be a place of participation, where we all find our part to play with our individual gifts and talents.

Yes, building into people's lives takes time, but we must take people from the place of entitlement to the place of empowerment, away from the feed-me and fix-me mode so many seem stuck in. As Paul wrote to the Ephesians of the first century:

Ephesians 4:11-12

So Christ himself gave the apostles, the prophets, the evangelists, the pastors and teachers, to equip his people for works of service, so that the body of Christ may be built up.

Father, I pray that as we lead a new generation, we will have the heart of a true leader. I pray that, as leaders, we will maintain a viable spiritual influence upon those potential leaders who need us to be strong and on the edge in our faith. May we always be changeable as the world changes and as times change.

Father, I pray that just as the sons of Issachar knew the seasons and the times, that we, as leaders, will know the season and timing to impart and develop a generation, recognizing that we can influence relationships with Your love and Your wisdom.

Lord, may we rise up to be transformers, not only transforming ourselves, but also transforming and influencing the other people in spheres we walk in. I pray for the Elijahs to rise up, Lord, for the Pauls to rise up, and that we would be one with You, Lord, in all that we do.

**In Jesus' name,
Amen!**

PEOPLE ARE NOT BORN GREAT LEADERS, ONLY BOYS AND GIRLS. THE LORD MOLDS AND MAKES THE HEARTS OF HIS LEADERS IN THE FURNACE OF ADVERSITY!

Chapter 6

Needed Leadership Skills

Matthew 5:9

> *Blessed be the peacemakers,*
> *for they will be called children of God.*

In this chapter, I want to share with you the importance of leadership skills, developing those skills as a necessary tool to the success of your own leadership and then recognizing those skills in those you are mentoring and discipling. Developing good leadership skills takes time. Without the necessary investment of time, very few people will have the skills to become the great leaders they want to be and are called to be. What follows are a few teachings from my monthly Covenant Leadership meetings. They are practical leadership skills with a spiritual focus.

1. CONFLICT RESOLUTION (RESOLVING CONFLICT RATIONALLY AND EFFECTIVELY)

We are called, as children of God, to be peacemakers. In many cases, conflict in the workplace just seems to be a fact of life. We have all seen situations where different people with different goals and needs have come into conflict, and we have also witnessed the often-intense personal animosity that can result.

The fact that conflict exists, however, is not necessarily a bad thing. As long as it is resolved effectively, conflict can lead to personal and professional growth. The only way to avoid conflict is to be a hermit. In many cases, effective conflict resolution skills can make the difference between positive and negative outcomes. The good news is that by resolving conflict successfully you can solve many of the problems that it has brought to the surface, as well as gain other benefits that you might not expect. Such benefits include:

Increased Understanding: The discussion needed to resolve conflict expands people's awareness of the situation, giving them an insight into how they can achieve their own goals without undermining those of other people.

Increased Unity: When conflict is resolved effectively, team members can develop stronger mutual respect and a renewed faith in their ability to work together.

Improved Self-Knowledge: Conflict pushes individuals to examine their goals in close detail, helping them to understand the things that are most important to them, sharpening their focus and enhancing their effectiveness.

However, if conflict is not handled effectively, the results can be damaging. Conflicting goals can quickly turn into personal dislike, and teamwork breakdowns, and talent is wasted, as people disengage from their work. It is easy to end up in a vicious downward spiral of negativity and recrimination.

Styles of Conflict Management

There are many different styles for conflict management and resolution. Much more important than the style or method, is your attitude and your heart relationships with people. Your style needs to suit yourself, your personality, the individuals involved and the situation and conflict you are trying to resolve. Here are some helpful pointers:

Needed Leadership Skills

1. Pick your battles.
2. Don't avoid resolution because of fear of bringing people together.
3. Keep your heart right.
4. Don't choose sides and don't play favorites because of relationship or personal experience.
5. Don't pre-judge.
6. Know your objective.
7. Make eye contact.
8. Listen first, talk second.
9. Be careful of your body language.
10. Select a good location. When possible, a neutral, inoffensive location and environment is best.
11. Choose your words carefully, such as "I understand you are feeling that way." "I can see why you feel that way." "I can see why you would be upset by this: HOWEVER ..." The objective is not to create conflict or avoid conflict, but rather to resolve conflict. Let the individuals involved know that you care.
12. Don't compromise your morals or integrity for the sake of agreement. In most cases, there are three sides to every story, and at least three sides to every conflict. Be sure that you are not picking *his* side or *her* side, but the Lord's

side. The solution is usually somewhere in the middle.

13. Avoid unnecessary interruptions. Privacy is important.

14. Resolution and compromise can normally only be achieved when you have allowed the dignity of the individuals involved to remain intact.

15. Keep the conflicts focused on the problems, and avoid personal attacks by all parties.

One of the relatively new elements that often causes conflicts is what people are saying online, in a blog, on Facebook or in some other public forum. Here are some steps that can be helpful in resolving such conflict:

1. Set a time and place for discussion. In most cases, online conflict happens in posts and comments between bloggers or contributors. This is something I actually enjoy (if done well), but it is also something of a problem for constructive resolution (due to its public nature and the fact that the conflict rarely stays between two people). If a comment thread is becoming destructive, I generally attempt to

take the discussion to a more private setting, either via email or text. Doing this tends to take the sting out of the interaction. Also, to set up a discussion for some point in the future helps to give each party a little space to calm down and approach the interaction more reasonably.

2. Define the problem or issue of disagreement, Many online conflicts tend to spill out into related topics, to the point that parties end up not really remembering what they're fighting about in the first place. Attempting to keep a discussion to one main point (at a time) can mean you're more likely to move through it and then tackle other issues.

3. Try to define how each contributes to the problem. Conflict is rarely a result of one person solely being at fault in a situation. Communicating to each other, not only what the other person has done wrong, but identifying your own failings in the case, can be a humbling experience, and usually brings you much closer to resolving the issue.

4. List past attempts to resolve the issue that were not successful. As online conflicts don't usually come out of longer-term relationships, this might not be as relevant. However there

are occasions where the same issues surface again and again, and it can be helpful to identify previous occasions and look at what the resolution attempt was. Identifying patterns of conflict can be quite illuminating (you might just learn a thing or two about yourself in the process).

5. Brainstorm, listing all possible solutions. When people fight, they generally push one argument or solution upon others and are not willing to entertain the idea that there might be other possible solutions. Listing the alternative opinions and solutions can help both parties to find a compromise.

6. Discuss and evaluate these possible solutions. Talking over the alternatives in a neutral and objective way helps both parties to see the pros and cons of different ways of thinking. This is where assertiveness and active listening skills come to the forefront.

7. Agree on a solution to try. In some cases, there is no solution needed (other than to agree to disagree and to move on). However, in other cases, there might be more. Agreeing on how and when to finish the conflict is important and stops those lingering wars where neither

party is willing to let the other one have the final word.

8. Agree on how each individual will work toward the solution. If there is some sort of agreement on the resolution, to agree on how each person will contribute to it is important so that there will be accountability for results or a lack of results.

9. Set up another meeting to discuss your progress. I actually find that when you have had an online conflict with someone and have moved to some point of resolution, it can be helpful to privately contact the person later on to debrief on it and see if there is any further resolution needed.

10. Reward each other as you each contribute toward the solution. Positive affirmations go a long way in all types of relationships, and. in resolving online conflicts, it is just as important.

I want to finish this section by again restating the truths that conflict is not necessarily a bad thing and can actually become a good thing. Personally I see conflict as an opportunity to grow.

2. TEAMWORK DEVELOPMENT SKILLS

Teamwork is "the coordination of organized effort or cooperation, creating a spirit of cooperation and unity." Teamwork means focusing our energies, efforts, ideas, initiatives and talents on mutual goals or objectives. A leader is the key coordinator.

Unity is the foundation of the universe we live in, the fundamental principle of harmony. Everything is working in cooperation with everything else, which produces results.

There is no such thing as a "self-made" man or woman. We can only truly reach our goals with the help of many others. The Bible clearly teaches:

Psalm 133:1

> *How good and pleasant it is*
> *when God's people live together in unity!*

Jesus' prayer in John 17 was for unity:

John 17:21-22

> *That they all may be one; as thou, Father, art*
> *in me, and I in thee, that they also may be one*
> *in us: that the world may believe that thou hast*

*sent me. And the glory which thou gavest me
I have given them; that they may be one, even
as we are one.*

The prophet Joel declared:

Joel 2:7
> *They charge like warriors;
>   they scale walls like soldiers.
> They all march in line,
>   not swerving from their course.*

This is unity. The days for the Lone Ranger are over.

The older and more experienced I get in life, the less I listen and base my decisions on what people say, but rather on what they do and produce. The following are categories which people typically fall into:

- **The dreamers:** He or she dreams but does nothing about it.
- **The doers:** These take the visions or dreams (their own and others) and turn them into money.
- **The true visionaries, leaders, achievers:** These are the ones who put inspiration and

perspiration, faith and action together to produce tangible results, reaching their goals and achieving their destiny. This requires teamwork.

Dwight D. Eisenhower defined *leader* as "getting someone else to do something you want done because he or she wants to do it." John C. Maxwell wrote, "A leader is one who knows the way, goes the way, and shows the way." Ronald Reagan said, "The greatest leader is not necessarily the one who does the greatest things ... but the one who motivates and gets others to do the greatest things." It's all about teamwork.

Here are eleven steps to teamwork:

1. Embrace the vision as your own.
2. Prefer one another and the team over self.
3. Don't lose your focus and responsibility and how it fits into the larger picture.
4. Take the initiative, don't procrastinate.
5. Just do it.
6. Foster unity and harmony in all that you do.
7. Don't be overly critical of others.
8. Don't sow seeds of doubt.
9. Set priorities that match your goals.

10. Be self motivated.
11. Don't quit.

3. TIME MANAGEMENT AND ORGANIZATIONAL SKILLS

I've been in leadership for going on fifty years now—in sports, coaching, business and ministry—and the one leadership style that I have adopted over the years, as noted, has been mentoring leadership. One of the key skills that must be developed in this style of leadership is management and organization. Again, this includes delegation, which requires and enhances personal and corporate discipline.

Some readers may know me on a more personal basis and know that I and other members of my family suffered from what we know today as ADD. This made the need for me to learn these skills more important, if I truly desired to be successful.

If you're a carpenter, you'd better learn how to use a hammer and a saw. If you're a programmer, you'd better understand how to use and operate your computer. If you're a plumber, learn how to torque your wrench. And, if you're a painter, learn how to stroke and what brush to use. If you're a leader you'd better learn how to use the tools of the trade, particularly those tools that will help you to manage, organize and delegate.

There are tools that can help you with time management. Learn to use them well. They are:

- To-Do Lists
- Planners
- Calendars
- DayTimers
- Goal Sheets
- PowerPoint Presentations
- Spreadsheets

It is not enough just to have these. You must learn to use them in an effective and regimented manner.

During the holidays one year, I had a very disappointing personal experience that challenged me to my core and pointed out to me how very important this subject is for all of us. I was visiting my sister in Pennsylvania, and when I left, I forgot to take my Planner. I called and asked her to mail it to me, and she did. But it took nineteen days to reach me, and during that time, I experienced frustration, confusion, a lower level of efficiency, and it all had a negative effect on my productivity.

What am I trying to say? I know beyond a shadow of a doubt that if you learn how to utilize these tools, you will become more productive, more at peace, better organized and a much better leader.

If someone is to be *my* leader and I choose to follow them, I want them to know where they're going. I'm not talking about their long-term vision. I mean on a daily, weekly and monthly basis.

Personally, I don't want to live my life, holding my finger in the dike because of the arrival of an unexpected flood, or continually putting out fires that erupt, just reacting to each current crisis. I want to be a leader who is personally disciplined and structured. I haven't arrived where I want to be yet, but I'm working at it every single day. I believe that this year I will be a better and more productive leader than I was last year. How about you?

Father, I pray that we may be a people who walk with crafted skills and with increased understanding to resolve conflict, to help others and to be able to give them insight as to how they can achieve their goals. And may we work in unity, knowing that this is Your heart.

Lord, I pray for wisdom for all leaders

and potential leaders reading this book to have the God-given ability to hear and identify issues, to be able to bring account-ability and resolution, and to understand that these are opportunities for all of us to grow and increase in wisdom.

In Jesus' name,
Amen!

OUR TRUE DESTINY CAN ONLY BE FOUND IN THE HANDS AND HEART OF GOD, BUT OUR LEGACY WILL BE FOUND THROUGH THE HANDS AND HEARTS OF OUR SONS AND DAUGHTERS!

Chapter 7

Making Decisions and Determining Directions

1 Kings 18:21, AMP

How long will you hesitate between two opinions?

Decision-making is key to the direction and impact of a leader. It is not just the method that each leader uses to arrive at decisions that is important. Even more important is how decisive that leader is. And, once a decision is made, how solid is that leader in his or her determination to stay the course? Do they also have the strength, should the need arise, to change their course of direction? Do they have the strength and character to admit an error?

As I said in ending the previous chapter, in my own life, I would not follow someone who didn't know where they were going or who was constantly double-minded about daily decisions. I follow only those who dare to believe and act on that belief.

THE MAN WHO DARES

The man who decides what he wants to achieve
And works till his dreams come true,
The man who will alter his course when he must
And bravely begin something new,
The man who's determined to make his world better
Who's willing to learn and to lead,
The man who keeps trying and doing his best,
Is the man who knows how to succeed.

The following information on decision-making may help you better understand some of the necessary mechanics and methods. As a leader, the key is to be decisive, confident and determined, but also open to change when necessary.

God said through Moses:

Deuteronomy 30:19-20, NLT
Today I have given you the choice between life and death, between blessings and curses. Now

I call on heaven and earth to witness the choice you make. Oh, that you would choose life, so that you and your descendants might live! You can make this choice by loving the LORD your God, obeying Him, and committing yourself firmly to Him. This is the key to your life. And if you love and obey the LORD, you will live long in the land sworn to your ancestors, Abraham, Isaac and Jacob.

Paul tells us in First Corinthians:

1 Corinthians 6:2-3, NLT

Don't you realize that someday we believers will judge the world? And since you are going to judge the world, can't you decide even these little things among yourselves? Don't you realize that we will judge angels? So you should surely be able to resolve ordinary disputes in this life.

And we see in Deuteronomy:

Deuteronomy 29:29, KJ21

The secret things belong to the LORD our God; but those things that are revealed belong to us

and to our children forever, so that we may do
all the words of the law.

The Power of One Good Decision

One good decision can reverse a lifetime of bad decisions. Your decisions weigh heavily, as they determine outcome. Leadership is the process of making and implementing such decisions. One part of your ministry is "feed" and the other is "lead." This includes decision-making.

All decisions fall into three categories: good, bad and "no" decisions (procrastinating). A non-decision is a bad decision. For this reason, Elijah asked the people of his day, *"How long will you halt and limp between two opinions?"* (AMPC).

To help you make decisions, first prepare a list of personal and ministry core values. Then, after you have made it, begin to act upon it. Stick to it and only alter it when you are shown something new.

What is a Good Decision?

A good decision is based on the Scriptures and the leading of God's Spirit. It is neither hasty, nor fearful and follows your core values and calling. To emphasize:

- A good decision is based on the wisdom of the Scriptures.
- A good decision is based on the witness of the Spirit.
- A good decision is neither hasty nor fearful. If we are fearful, we will not take action.
- A good decision is based on your values. When you know your core values (honesty, purity, frugality, etc.) then a great percentage of your decisions are already made for you.
- A good decision is something that is based on your calling. What may be a good idea for others could be a very bad "fit" for your future.

What Is a Bad Decision?

A bad decision is based upon emotions (fear, frustration, anger or depression, for example) and/or outward appearances. It is short-term and speculative. An example can be seen in Song of Solomon 3:2. For this woman, it was a bad decision to go out into the streets at night. Only a certain type of woman did that. Therefore, she risked being mistaken for a woman of the night.

To emphasize:

- A bad decision is anything based on fear. Fear brings haste and panic.
- A bad decision is anything based on appearances. Eve ate the fruit from the tree because it looked so good.
- A bad decision is anything based on the short-term realities. You must be prepared to face long-term consequences.
- A bad decision is anything based on emotions (frustration, anger or depression).

What Is a "No" Decision?

- I am making a "no" decision when I postpone a decision because of feelings and/or friendships, fear of error, overconfidence or running from responsibility.
- I make a "no" decision when my feelings of friendship gets in the way of doing what is right (some people cannot grow or go with you to the next level).
- I am making a "no" decision when my fear of making a wrong move paralyzes me until others end up making decisions for me. When I am filled with remorse and regret, I will make no decision for fear of making a wrong one. This will cause me to quickly change back and

forth numerous times, as each position makes me insecure.

- I make a "no" decision when I don't want the responsibility of leadership and prefer to be told what to do. A good leader calls the shots and then takes the shots, if necessary.
- I make a "no" decision when I am over-confident that I have plenty of time to decide, and so I procrastinate until my opinions are meaningless.

2 Corinthians 1:17, NASB

Therefore, I was not vacillating when I intended to do this, was I? Or what I purpose, do I purpose according to the flesh, so that with me there will be yes, yes and no, no at the same time?

What is a decision? It is a choice of direction, a purpose, a resolve. Paul was a decisive person. He never said "yes" and "no" at the same time. He realized the importance of not being fickle or vacillating in his decisions.

There are three very important areas of decision-making in leadership: financial, relational and transitional.

Financial Decisions

- *"Should I spend it?"* Is this purchase a part of my budget? Some churches only operate on 70% of their income. Don't spend everything your beady eyes are looking at. Live on 80-90%.

- *"Should I save it?"* Is this purchase a part of my overall financial plan? Am I ready for depression or recession? Cash is king. As the saying goes, "Can what you get and get what you can."

- *"Should I seed it?"* Has God given me this seed to create a greater harvest? Churches should tithe and also give offerings.

- *"Is it honest and above board?"* Money is a test of honesty. Any effort to cover up, misappropriate or deceive is not only unethical but may be criminal.

- *"Is there a conflict of interest?"* This question relates to money, gifts, business partnerships, multi-level operations and members. Could I rebuke them if needed? Does it benefit the person or organization?

- *"Am I pushing?"* For example, taking three offerings in a single service.

- *"Who is in charge?"* Do I have freedom with accountability and counsel from gifted advisors? The senior leader has to be the one in charge and must be able to make decisions with ac-countability.

Relational Decisions
- Personality? Is it a good fit or a disaster?
- Character?
- Five-fold calling? Is their gift a good match? What are they? Do a credit rating or run a check on them.
- Performance? Do they walk fast or slow?
- Attitude? Will they staple papers or whatever else you need them to do? They must be both willing and humble.
- Motives? Is this a stepping stone for themselves? Do they have a personal agenda? What is it?
- Commitment? Is this a son or daughter or a hireling? A son or daughter is more interested in the growth of the house, but a hireling is in it for some personal advantage.

Transitional Decisions

James 1:8, GNT

If you are like that, unable to make up your mind and undecided in all you do, you must not think that you will receive anything from the Lord.

NLT

Their loyalty is divided between God and the world, and they are unstable in everything they do.

MSG

Adrift at sea, keeping all your options open.

Decisions involve transitions. A decision is basically a transition from where you are to where you want to be. If a dream is to go anywhere, a decision must be made. The strength of your decision determines the strength of your discipline.

Personal Areas of Transition for Ministers

1. **Physical:** You need to make a decision to work out, to eat right, to get off of certain medications and lose weight. *"For physical training is of some value, but godliness has value for all things, holding promise for both the present life and the life to come"* (1 Timothy 4:8).
2. **Career:** You need to make decisions that will advance your education, move you into a dif-

ferent ministry or change priorities. *"There is a time for everything and a season for every activity under heaven"* (Ecclesiastes 3:1).

3. **Financial:** You need to make decisions to live within your means and get out of debt and to bring the church out from under financial stress, no matter what the cost. *"Let no debt remain outstanding"* (Romans 13:8).

4. **Spiritual:** You need to make a decision concerning your personal devotional habits, sermon preparation and your moral purity. *"As newborn babes, desire the pure milk of the Word, that you may grow thereby"* (1 Peter 2:2, NKJV). *"Devote yourself to prayer"* (Colossians 4:2).

5. **Family:** You need to make a decision to develop a closer relationship with your spouse and children. *"Don't you see that children are God's best gifts"* (Psalm 127:3, MSG).

6. **Schedule:** You must make a decision to have enough rest time in your schedule and must prioritize the important over the urgent. Limit time wasters like video games, Internet surfing and phone doodling. You need a full day for message preparation. It is important to make a daily, weekly and monthly schedule and make

sure your schedule is accomplished. *"Making the most of your time, because the days are evil"* (Ephesians 5:16, EHV).

7. **Relationships**: You need to make a decision to pour yourself in discipleship into certain relationships and also to cut off others. *"Of course, your former friends are surprised when you no longer plunge into the flood of wild and destructive things they do. So they slander you"* (1 Peter 4:4, NLT).

FOCUS AND FUNCTION

I will end this chapter talking about focus and function, because after you make a decision the most important thing is to focus on it and function in it, so as to implement your plans.

First, Focus

Luke 9:62, NKJV

But Jesus said to him, "No one, having put his hand to the plow, and looking back, is fit for the Kingdom of God."

I believe the present primary attack of the enemy against leaders and potential leaders is distraction and division. Don't be distracted by the season, by others, by entertainment, or by personal desires (lusts):

Galatians 5:16

So I say, walk by the Spirit, and you will not gratify the desires of the flesh.

A critical component of effective leaders is that they are focused. They detest distractions and anything that would hinder effective performance. Sometimes, because of it, they can be seen as being impatient and intolerant. They may seem to be extremely driven, but that is not a character flaw. It is an internal mechanism that propels them to achieve their intended objective.

Personal discipline is essential to leadership. You simply cannot be an effective leader if you don't have some discipline in your life. After all, you are a role model for others. People are watching you and looking for discipline as the essence of your life. Personal discipline, or self-discipline, then, is an essential quality of an authentic leader. Without it, you cannot gain the respect of your followers.

Then, Function

For a leader, the vision must always be before you, and you must be working to bring it to pass.

James 2:26

> *Faith without works is dead.*

You must know your ministry vision and mission, so they must be clearly defined. The vision of a leader is powerful because he or she believes in the vision and mission. Theirs is not just a statement framed on a wall. They not only believe it; they live it every single day—in the workplace, at home and at church.

Set and periodically update your personal goals and objectives. Be properly rested and prepared for whatever your ministry function is, remembering that fatigue is your enemy.

Know that there is life in the power of your tongue:

Proverbs 18:21

> *The tongue has the power of life and death,*
> *and those who love it will eat its fruit.*

Learn to speak good things to yourself and to others. In this way, motivate and inspire the people your are leading.

Understand proper alignment and authority and learn to walk in it.

Joel 2:7, NKJV

They run like mighty men,
They climb the wall like men of war;
Everyone marches in formation,
And they do not break ranks.

Joel was describing God's end-time army. These men and women will climb the walls like mighty warriors, and they will not break ranks. The officers being raised up in this hour will know who they are in Christ and also who Christ is in them. They will know the power and authority that has been God-given, and also the authority that has been delegated, and will understand how to rightly relate and connect in covenant with those God has called them to lead.

In the New Testament story of the centurion, the man, when speaking to the Lord Jesus, revealed that he was a man who understood authority. He understood it because, as he said, he was *"a man under authority"* (Matthew 8:9, KJV). The fullness of power in any man or woman's life will not be truly realized until they understand and walk in proper alignment and authority.

As I have noted, it has been my privilege to be discipled and mentored in sports, business and ministry by men and women who cared about me, corrected me and were the kind of role models I could work with, look up to and submit to. That makes all the difference.

It's all about faith, focus and function. Let's learn to work this out in unity and harmony. None of us is meant to be independent, and it is not healthy for us to be codependent. Instead, we must be interconnected and interrelated. Respecting the gift of God and positioning that God has established in each of our lives is important to our destiny.

Father, I pray that those who read this will become men and women of God who have the mind of Christ. I pray for clear thinking and supernatural clarity to make decisions and move forward in all that they do. I ask for an impartation of Your wisdom, Lord, so that everyone who is impacted by their decisions will benefit. I pray that the result of their decision-making would chart a course in their life toward their destiny and those they are to lead.

I pray for strength for them to follow through and function in their decisions and choices. I also pray for supernatural strength when they are weak, to make the decisions based on the high call which is on their lives.

In Jesus' name,
Amen!

————— A Thought to Remember —————

MANY HAVE BECOME CRITICAL OF THE CHURCH, BUT LET US NEVER FORGET THAT THE LORD IS MADLY IN LOVE WITH THE CHURCH, HIS BRIDE!

Chapter 8

THE PLACE OF
Research and Development, Marketing and Promotions

Proverbs 29:18, KJV

Where there is no vision, the people perish: but he that keepeth the law, happy is he.

I wouldn't want to be employed by a company who was not willing to invest a significant portion of its resources into research and development, marketing and promotions. Why? Because I don't want to be involved with some dead-end venture. This is what happens when people eat their seed instead of sowing it. They end up with a full belly but nothing left for the future.

We need to sow, not just into the church, and not just into our businesses, and also not just into our families; we need to sow into our own personal lives, so that we can obtain the maximum effect and the desired results. One of the ways I can recognize the outlook and attitude of a company, ministry or individual is their willingness to sow into themselves for the future.

For a number of years, I fell into a bit of a religious ditch (and a ditch is nothing more than a grave without ends). My stagnation began with a very simple statement, something like, "If it is God, then you don't need to promote it," or "we're not promoting anything," which, in and of itself, is fine, but before you know it, the Spirit of Religion has attached itself to it and brought condemnation.

In that flat statement, "If it is God, then you don't need to promote it," lies a spiritual truth, but does that mean that we never make a brochure, share a testimony, invite someone to an event, promote or recommend a CD, DVD or any other resource item? The woman who met Jesus at the well in Samaria could not stop talking about Him to her friends and neighbors. If it was good enough for her to promote Jesus, then it is certainly okay with me too. It is important that we do all things according to the Word of God, but that Word urges us to spread the Good News any possible way we can.

Some say, "We're not building the Church; we're building the Kingdom," but when you build the Church, you *are* building the Kingdom. I need to make disciples, not converts. And in order to make good disciples, I need to rightly connect them to the Church (the Body of Christ) through some sort of promotional means.

There are many expressions of what the Church is: fellowships, ministries, a nucleus and an extension. Part of the purpose of us having church is to develop a support system made up of Christian believers to stand together against the attempts of the enemy and the circumstances that confront us. It is in that family and corporate setting that we can find the strength to live the life of a true disciple of Christ.

Some people say, "Well, that is church and not business," but I say, "The church is to be about the Father's business." As every leader in the Body of Christ knows or will come to know, there is a business aspect to the work of the church—if and when we get serious about extending and advancing the Kingdom. That's where research and development come in.

Research and development involves understanding the particular product or service you are providing and finding ways to improve it, prepare it, and present it to potential consumers or users. This must be done in a favorable setting and manner so that the benefits of it are clearly understood.

On an individual basis, if a person is not reading, studying, gathering information and understanding—all for the purpose of personal self-improvement and development—I have a problem with that individual. It will be only a matter of time before they hit a dead-end. Therefore, we must break off some of the stereotypes and the condemnation men would heap upon us. The Lord of the Harvest is calling us to partner with Him in that harvest. And this includes promotions.

God, therefore, wants us to excel. He wants us to have the maximum impact that we can in extending and advancing His Kingdom and in building the Body of Christ (the Church). He wants us to be good stewards of the resources, gifts, talents, abilities, ministries and callings He has given us.

How can we do marketing and promotions?

1. WE PROMOTE CHRIST JESUS

Philippians 3:3-4

For it is we who are the circumcision, we who serve God by His Spirit, who boast in

Christ Jesus, and who put no confidence in the flesh–though I myself have reasons for such confidence.

Any means that we find available to us that promotes Christ and His principles should be taken advantage of.

2. OUR FIRST MEANS OF PROMOTION IS OUR PERSONAL TESTIMONY

Revelation 12:11

*They triumphed over him
by the blood of the Lamb
and by the word of their testimony;
they did not love their lives so much
as to shrink from death.*

Nothing speaks louder to the world around us than a life well lived in Christ. Let your light shine that men might see your good works and glorify your Father (see Matthew 5:16).

3. WE MUST KNOW HOW TO CONVEY THE VISION

Proverbs 29:18, KJV

Where there is no vision, the people perish: but
he that keepeth the law, happy is he.

We are called, not just to live the Christian life before others, but to share our experience with as many as we can. The first way we do that is by sharing our testimony. Let's talk about Jesus.

4. THROUGH ANY MEANS AVAILABLE TO US, WE MARKET AND PROMOTE JESUS

As with any marketing and promotion, the most important element is casting the vision. The product is irrelevant and interchangeable. We have the most wonderful product to share—eternal life through Christ.

- **First Base**: Prospecting and suspecting. Generating leads, qualifying contacts. Who are you casting your vision to?
- **Second Base**: Make your presentation clear: What? Who? Where? When? Why? Should it be visual?
- **Third Base**: Closing the deal, the invitation, asking for a commitment.

- **The Goal:** A soul saved, a satisfied congregant.

5. WHAT IS OUR VISION?

It it important to present the Lord and His Church in the best possible way. In the past, we have called the Church Pentecostal or Charismatic. The problem is that each of these names have long-standing stigmas attached to them. I suggest using the name Spirit Contemporary to describe the Church of today. What stigma could possibly be attached to that name?

What is a Spirit Contemporary church? It is a church that is full of the Spirit and spiritually relevant to our modern society and to the culture of our day and age.

6. REACHING OUT

Now that we know what to call it, we need to start reaching out to others. We can do this through the use of cards, flyers, brochures, posters, videos, and all other types of media—TV, radio, newspapers, the Internet, Facebook, Twitter, emails—you name it. Let's use it all.

The information we present through these various means of communication must be clearly written and easily readable and must contain your main points of interest.

Who do we reach out to? To any personal contacts we might have. Often we can begin by reaching out to the sick, the imprisoned, the troubled, the hungry, the poor, the needy. People who find themselves in these categories are often very open to the Gospel. But don't stop there. Reach out to anyone and everyone.

Often, the members of our congregations will know people in need of our help, people in need of the Gospel. That's an excellent place to start.

Again, think about the woman Jesus met at the well in Samaria:

John 4:39-42

> *Many of the Samaritans from that town believed in him because of the woman's testimony, "He told me everything I ever did." So when the Samaritans came to him, they urged him to stay with them, and he stayed two days. And because of his words many more became believers. They said to the woman, "We no longer believe just because of what you said; now we have heard for ourselves, and we know that this man really is the Savior of the world."*

7. FOR PROMOTIONAL PURPOSES, WE MUST DEVELOP CENTERS OF INFLUENCE IN THE COMMUNITY

In these centers, we will first convince a core group of their need for salvation. Then we will train them to reach out to others. And thus we will multiply our efforts exponentially.

Teach all of your disciples that their mission in life is to reach others. Help them to see that in helping others they will fulfill their own destinies.

Before we close this chapter, here is a simple list of dos and don'ts of promotions and marketing.

SOME DOS AND DON'TS OF PROMOTIONS AND MARKETING

1. Focus on what you have, not on what you *don't* have.
2. Market and promote your assets and vision.
3. Avoid using stereotypes and Christianese language.
4. Take a broad-based approach.
5. In this way, give God something to bless like He did the loaves and fishes.
6. Utilize your whole team.
7. Emphasize your strengths and values.

Research and Development, Marketing and Promotions

Marketing, promotions, research and development are all important elements in looking to the future. God's will for each of us is that we continue to grow and develop in Him. These elements are especially important in the life of a leader, ministry or business that wants to be a forerunner, one that is on the edge, always pioneering, always pressing toward the future, to what is happening now and what is happening next.

This leads me to this next chapter that I think will bless you—Being a Forerunner.

Lord, bless this people with the knowledge that we have the most wonderful thing to offer the men and women of our modern world. Salvation in Jesus has not grown stale at all. And we all need it to live a victorious life in this twenty-first century.

Teach us to be wise in the methods we use to promote You and Your Church, and give us a harvest of souls to lay at Your feet.

In Jesus' name,
Amen!

END-TIME LEADERS MUST BE PREPARED TO LEAD AT THE SPEED OF CHANGE, ON THE EDGE OF CHAOS, ON THE PROPHETIC EDGE!

Chapter 9

Being a Forerunner

Isaiah 62:10, KJV

Go through, go through the gates; prepare ye the way of the people; cast up, cast up the highway; gather out the stones; lift up a standard for the people.

What is a forerunner? *Forerunner* can be defined as:

1. Predecessor; ancestor; forbear; precursor.
2. An omen, sign or indication of something to follow; portent: the warm evenings were a forerunner of summer.
3. A person who goes or is sent in advance to announce the coming of someone or something that follows; herald; harbinger.
4. The forerunner, John the Baptist.

A forerunner is a visionary, one who sees the future and works to bring it into the present. Forerunners are characterized by their motivation to build, create, innovate and reform whatever they are engaged in.

There are forerunners with a wide range of interest, talents, and social perspectives. Although the following is not an exhaustive list, it reveals some of the character traits a forerunner may exhibit:

A forerunner:
- Is motivated by values, vision and ideals.
- Is creative, approaching any task with optimism and expectation.
- Has a can-do attitude.
- Knows how to problem solve and is not intimidated by any problem.
- Is a non-conformer, a square peg who does his own thing.
- Is a dreamer and thinker.
- Is an outsider and loner who often doesn't belong to groups.
- Is willing to sacrifice for what he believes in.
- Is rarely engaged in something he doesn't believe in.

- Is often confrontational, whether skilled or not so skilled in the art of confrontation.
- Is motivated to build, fix and improve things.
- Is not easily manipulated by the media and pop culture of the day.
- Is a lover of change.
- Is motivated to excellence in everything he does.
- Is an early adopter. He gets a concept quickly and moves into something new very easily.
- Is a lover of adventure.
- Is often an excellent communicator (teachers, musicians, broadcasters, artists, authors, journalists, filmmakers) because he desires to influence and impact the world around him.

THE FORERUNNER GENERATION

For the past sixty years, the Western world has experienced a sustained technological revolution unlike anything in the past. Historically, after every technological revolution, there has come a social reformation following closely behind. Observation will reveal that business, science, government, education, media, entertainment, the arts and religion are all in various stages of reformation today. Considering the significance of the technological revolution, this could be the greatest social reformation in recorded history, and it is the forerunners who will lead it. Reformation and transformation is the passion and the ability of forerunners. The past forty years have been the era of the "techno-geek," and the next forty years will be the era of the "forerunner generation."

A forerunner goes before and enters into something new that God has and then intercedes for others to enter into it also. Forerunners are pioneers in the Kingdom of God. They are characterized by their motivation to reform the Body of Christ. Through grace and revelation, they are called to the ministry of preparing the Church for the Lord's return.

MORE PERSONALITY TRAITS OF A SPIRITUAL FORERUNNER

- He highly values being guided by the Holy Spirit.
- He is a non-conformer in lifestyle or some other aspect of his life.
- He does not value belonging and often avoids it. For this reason, he is often seen by others as an outsider.

- He has been or is being prepared for powerful ministry through a prolonged wilderness experience.
- He has made significant personal sacrifices for the sake of the Gospel.
- He has been misunderstood and often persecuted for his revelation of the Kingdom.
- He is not afraid to confront duplicity and sin, even when there are personal costs involved.
- He is focused on fulfilling his call and purpose in Christ.
- He loves and pursues the truths of the Gospel.
- He is not afraid of change.
- He is highly adventurous.

BEING EARLY ADOPTERS

Forerunners recognize the need for change and adopt it quickly and easily. They work for change through teaching, writing and demonstration. Martin Luther, John Wesley and Charles Finney were among the most well-known forerunners. Each of these men played a role in God's reformation of the Church. Many unknown men and women also recognized, supported and taught the reformation message, and thus spread it throughout the whole

Body of Christ. Forerunners see the path and are quick to evaluate, adopt and integrate new revelation into their lives and ministry.

FORERUNNERS IN THE SCRIPTURES

There were three forerunners identified as such in the Scriptures—Elijah, John the Baptist and Jesus, (who was "The Forerunner"). However, there were many others who did the ministry of a forerunner.

John the Baptist proclaimed a "preparation" before the coming of Jesus' ministry. Forerunners are concerned with preparation. Malachi asserted that God would send Elijah before the great and terrible Day of the Lord (see Malachi 4:5). Many scholars believe that the Lord will prepare His Bride for His return with a company of forerunners who will prepare and "make straight" the way of the Lord before His triumphant reunion with the Bride, His Church. These forerunner ministers will participate in bringing about the reformation and restoration of the Church.

A forerunner ministry is one of:
- Prophetic Intercession
- Prophetic Proclamation

- Prophetic Teaching and Preaching
- Ministry through the Words of Knowledge and of Wisdom

A forerunner ministry exposes and confronts:
- Hidden sin (bringing inner or physical healing)
- Useless traditions or dead religion
- Demonic strongholds
- Unbelief, idolatry and impure motives
- Worldliness

THE FORERUNNER ARMY

God is raising up an army of forerunners who will prepare the way of the Lord. The forerunner ministry is a catalyst in the coming together of this army into one trained and effective unit that will pull down every high place and lift up every low place and make a (high) way for the Lord (see Isaiah 10:3-5). Then all flesh will see the Glory of the Lord Jesus.

JOHN THE BAPTIST AND THE FORERUNNER MINISTRY

God has been speaking to us in these days about the wilderness in many different contexts. I want to share some insights into the wilderness ministry of John the Baptist, the Preparer of the Way, the Forerunner of the Lord.

Luke wrote of John the Baptist:

Luke 1:80, NAB(RE)

The child grew and became strong in spirit, and he was in the wilderness till the day of his manifestation to Israel.

From John's birth to the day of his manifestation was a long time—about thirty years. As the son of a priest, he had the right to be part of the religious system in Jerusalem, but God separated him from all of that, and kept him out in the wilderness. This wilderness time was, for John, a growing time, a time of becoming strong in the Spirit. During this time, John did not fret or strive. He did not yearn for the activities and the rites and forms of religion. He walked humbly and patiently with God and grew strong in spirit. If we have been called to a forerunner ministry, we, too, must expect and be willing to undergo a wilderness preparation. This means being removed from the hustle and bustle of the religious systems.

There, in the wilderness, John was an unknown, precluded from the religious scene, unrecognized, hidden and apparently unfruitful. Jerusalem was where it all happened. We, too, must be ready for such a time, and it may be quite a long time of hiddenness, with no evident ministry, nothing of what is seen as success, no recognition, but only a learning from God and an intimate walking with Him.

One day, however, the forerunner will come forth, and become visible and fruitful.

THE MANIFESTATION OF THE FORERUNNER

Luke 3:2

The Word of God came to John son of Zechariah
in the wilderness.

This was the next stage of John's life and ministry. When God's time was fulfilled (and not before), John was launched into his forerunner ministry by the Word of the Lord coming to him in the wilderness.

The Word of the Lord did not come to the religious leaders in Jerusalem or to the masses attending their services. The Word that came to John included the command to go into the region of the Jordan. It imparted to him what was to be the thrust of his message, namely the call to repentance and baptism, and it also revealed to him his role as *"The voice of one crying in the wilderness: 'Prepare the way of the Lord; Make straight in the desert A highway for our God' "* (Isaiah 40:3, NKJV). We, likewise, in the wilderness, out of the church systems, are to listen for the Word of the Lord. There will come a time of manifestation and of revelation to us about where to go, what to do and what to speak. That time will be of the Lord's choosing and appointment, and we must be ready to wait quietly and expectantly for it and not seek to contrive or hasten it.

THE MINISTRY OF THE FORERUNNER

In *Godet's* massive commentary on the Gospel of John, the writer gives, as one interpretation of the passage in John 10:1-6, that John the Baptist was the gatekeeper to the fold of Israel, who opened the door to Jesus, the Shepherd, to come in and to call out His sheep. The fold was the religious system of Judaism, and Jesus called His sheep out from the security of that system into His flock, where the security was no longer that of a system, but of His Person, as Shepherd.

The people came out to hear John, from Judea and Jerusalem, in a great move of the Spirit of God. John himself did not go to Jerusalem to seek out the people. Rather the residents of Jerusalem came looking for him, knowing that he had a message from God.

Then, for a time in John's ministry, it was, as they say, "all on." Crowds kept coming out to see him, and some of them gathered round him for a period as his disciples. But John's ministry was not to gather people to himself, but that of preparing the way of the Lord and of pointing men and women to Him.

After this very exciting time, John suddenly faded from the scene, his mission accomplished. Even his most intimate disciples and closest companions were now directed away from himself and to Jesus.

All this has its parallels in what I believe God is calling us to now. The day will come when those who have been receiving the Word of the Lord in the wilderness will become a voice crying, "Prepare the way for the Lord!" People, moved by the Spirit of God, will come, eager to hear.

They will be people who have come out from man's denominations and religious systems, as well as nonreligious people who are hungry for reality. At such a time, we may well be surrounded by many enquirers, and our task will be to call for repentance and to direct people to the Shepherd.

Jesus, the Good Shepherd and the Great Shepherd of the sheep, will call His own by name and will bring them out of the multiplied folds of Christendom into His personal flock. People's security will no longer be in the safety of an organized fold, but in the Person of Jesus, who is leading His flock.

All John had to do was prepare people to hear and follow Jesus. It was not his responsibility to tell folks to come out of the folds, nor is it ours. Jesus Himself will call His people out. Our role will simply be to be open the gates for Him.

WHEN THIS TIME COMES

When this time comes and a flood of people come out to us, there will be a strong temptation to gather them around ourselves, to establish fellowships or churches, but that temptation we must strongly and vehemently resist. Our ministry, as was John's, will be to urge people to repentance and then direct them to follow the Lord and Him only.

Jesus has said *"There will be ONE FLOCK and ONE SHEPHERD"* (John 10:16, Emphasis added). That is the vision which inspires us, the vision of the day when the religious structures and denominations will pass away, when Jesus will have

154

called His own sheep by name and led them out (see John 10:3). Then we shall all be simply sheep of His pasture.

A FINAL OBSERVATION

One final observation about John's ministry: The preparation time for it was long, and the ministry time was short (probably no more than a few months), but the consequences were eternal. Such are God's ways: much hiddenness, crucially-timed ministry and results that last forever!

Father, thank You for the ones who prepare the way, the ones You have chosen to clear the path before us, those who go before, where no man has gone. I pray that as one of them cries out in their own wilderness, "Make way for the Lord" (in a way that is uniquely for their current situation and location), that you will bless them and bless them abundantly.

I pray for a heightened supernatural understanding of their revelation and their vision, as they scout out new territories in the Spirit and in the land.

I pray for supernatural strength, endurance and patience for the forerunners You are raising up. May we, as leaders, recognize them, having eyes to see them, and help to cheer them on. Give them all the tools they need to accomplish Your desire in their lives. As leaders, may we have the wisdom required to spur them on to the next level.

In Jesus' name,
Amen!

THE CHURCH IS NOT A BUILDING, NOT A DENOMINATION AND NOT A FELLOWSHIP; IT IS GOD'S KINGDOM PEOPLE!

Chapter 10

Having the Spirit of a Leader

1 Chronicles 12:32, KJV

*And of the children of Issachar, which were men
who had understanding of the times, to know
what Israel ought to do; the heads of them were
two hundred, and all their brethren were at their
commandment.*

Leadership and the development of leaders is one
of the most complex and complicated processes in
discipleship. And this is an hour when God is calling
forth, positioning and preparing leaders, key labor-
ers for the harvest.

In the training and development of a leader, we
can talk about the foundation of leadership. We can
talk about what God is looking for in a leader. We
can also talk about the wisdom required to lead.

Having the Spirit of a Leader

The Bible tells us: *"wisdom is the principal thing"* (Proverbs 4:7, KJV). Solomon cried out for wisdom. Wisdom is much more valuable to a leader than silver and gold could ever be.

We can talk about the mechanics (tools, charts, graphs, to-do lists) or the focus and function of the leader or the other needed abilities and skills. To me, however, the most important aspect of leadership is the spirit of a leader—the actual anointing to lead.

This is an inherent quality of God in man that brings the process, that develops the hunger that stirs the perseverance. It is not something you can put your finger on or something you can either teach nor explain. It must come from God.

There is what I call the spirit of a leader, the anointing to lead, and when you are looking for a leader, this is an intangible factor, but you can almost taste it, feel it and sense it. You somehow just know that person is born to lead.

When the spirit of the leader is present, in and on a leader's life, there will be a natural attraction to follow them. That anointing will birth in the heart of a leader a sense and an understanding of the visionary realm. Consequently, they will see things the way they ought to be.

We can see this in the Scriptures with the sons of Issachar. They were born to lead. They had an anointing for leadership. Therefore they were able to go from vision to mission, to strategy, to action, and the children of Israel followed them. It was a natural thing brought on by the supernatural touch of God upon their lives.

Many people think of themselves as leaders and call themselves leaders. Many of them will tell you about their capabilities, their callings and their five-fold office. But if they don't have a following, then who are they leading? And how can they be a leader? True leadership attracts followers.

God knows the right timing in the life of every leader for them to begin to gather others to themselves. But the same hand that gathers is the hand that scatters. Jesus said that the way we would know a tree is by the fruit it bears. If there is an anointing or spirit to lead upon your life, the fruit of that will be followers. You don't start out that way, but it is the place you ultimately end up.

Oh, yes, there will be struggles, problems, twists and turns, and, at times it, will feel like your pathway is all uphill. But, ultimately, those who wait upon the Lord shall renew their strength (see

Isaiah 40:31), and the man or woman chosen by God to lead will see fruit in the form of followers.

THE IMPORTANCE OF ATTITUDE

The Bible is the blueprint for successful Christian living. God is practical, orderly and systematic. God declared to Joshua:

Joshua 1:8
> *Keep this Book of the Law always on your lips; meditate on it day and night, so that you may be careful to do everything written in it. Then you will be prosperous and successful.*

God wants us to be successful. He wants to show us how to be a good fathers, good sons, good husbands, good businessmen, good teachers, good friends and good soldiers. But your attitude will directly affect your altitude.

Do you have a positive mental attitude? Many times people will give this example: Is the glass half-full or half empty? But there is a whole lot more to having a positive attitude than just having an optimistic perception.

WHAT IS MY ATTITUDE?

Toward Myself

We must all develop a healthy self-image. Who do you think you are? Do you honestly like yourself? What could you do to change and improve your self-esteem and self-concept? A healthy self-worth is important.

For far too long Christians have been beating themselves up, not seeing themselves as God sees them. Refuse to focus on your weaknesses, your shortcomings, the obstacles you face or your fears. Instead, focus on your God and what He has said about you.

How does the Lord see us? As a winner and an overcomer in all circumstances. Somehow I have to learn to be happy, not only with the circumstances I am involved with, but also happy with who God made me in those circumstances. Paul wrote:

Philippians 4:11-13

> *I am not saying this because I am in need, for I have learned to be content whatever the circumstances. I know what it is to be in need, and I know what it is to have plenty. I have learned the secret of being content in any and every*

situation, whether well fed or hungry, whether living in plenty or in want. I can do all this through him who gives me strength.

Toward Others

My perception of self affects my perception of others. Do I find myself critical or judgmental of others? Do I lack compassion and understanding when I am dealing with others? Am I willing to prefer others, especially in team settings? Am I looking at the vision and looking at the fulfillment of the vision, without having to worry about who receives the credit for it? Learn to love others as God loves them, and that will change everything.

Toward Leadership

Are my views toward leadership overly affected by negative past experiences with people in authority in my life? Do I hear myself commenting concerning leadership as if it were something or someone apart? For example, do I say, "Leadership said" or "leadership wants" when I'm dealing with people I'm trying to lead. Am I using third-party references? Is it us or them, we or they?

How do I receive correction? Do I have a tendency to react or respond? Do I receive it as constructive or as condemning and personal? As a leader, I obviously want to be liked. But when I am dealing with those I am leading, real love has to be willing to confront and lay aside my need to be loved and accepted and put the future and progress of others first. Is my attitude right in this regard?

About Change

"Oh no! Not more change!" Everything about being a Christian or being a leader is about change. Change, transition and transformation ... that's what the Christian life is all about.

Romans 12:1-2

> *Therefore, I urge you, brothers and sisters, in view of God's mercy, to offer your bodies as a living sacrifice, holy and pleasing to God—this is your true and proper worship. Do not conform to the pattern of this world, but be transformed by the renewing of your mind. Then you will be able to test and approve what God's will is—his good, pleasing and perfect will.*

Am I willing to allow God to change the way I think and the way I feel, to actually transform my mind, so that His perfect will can be manifest through me? The change must first come in my thoughts before it can come om deeds.

Proverbs declares:

Proverbs 23:7, KJV
For as he [a man] thinketh in his heart, so is he.

One of the strangest secrets is this: what I become is what I think about most. It's time to start thinking about what I am thinking about. If I can let God transform my mind, He can transform my life. I have to stop my "stinking thinking" and develop an attitude of true faith.

Be more careful of your words and your thoughts now than ever. They are powerful. For instance, avoid saying things like this:

- Nothing good ever happens to me.
- I'll never be successful.
- I just don't have what it takes.
- I'll never get out of this mess.
- This thing is killing me.

It's time to bury *if* and *can't* and know that I can do a thing if I think I can.

IF YOU THINK YOU'RE BEATEN

If you think you're beaten, you are,
If you think you dare not, you don't.
If you would like to win, but think you can't,
It's almost for sure you won't.

If you think your losing, you've lost.
For out in the world we find –
Success begins with a person's will.
It's all in the state of mind.

If you think you're outclassed, you are.
You've got to think high to rise.
You have to stay with it,
In order to win the prize.

Life's battles don't always go,
To the one with the better plan.
For more often than not, you will win,
If only you think you can.

Sooner or later, a man or woman has to step out and dare to be different, dare to be great and dare to do something important. The sweetest fruit is usually near the trunk of the tree, but we have to go out on a limb, and that is the heart of the man or woman who dares.

I have to deal with my own heart and my own mind. Using the blood of Jesus, I can cast out spirits, but Paul talks about pulling down the strongholds of thought:

2 Corinthians 10:3-5, KJV

> *For though we walk in the flesh, we do not war after the flesh: (for the weapons of our warfare are not carnal, but mighty through God to the pulling down of strong holds;) casting down imaginations, and every high thing that exalteth itself against the knowledge of God, and bringing into captivity every thought to the obedience of Christ.*

Because of being a leader and walking in leadership, I must walk in my objectives. But, at the same time, I must be willing to be flexible and ready to change. I also cannot allow myself the luxury of being upset about things. When we lead on the edge of chaos and in the midst of change, how we react and how we respond will be closely monitored by those who follow us. Get an attitude adjustment!

About Setbacks or Failures

Some of the most successful people in the world have also experienced great failures and setbacks. I personally have not met many successful people who met with great success on their first attempt.

Setbacks and failures are two different things. Life is full of setbacks, obstacles and hindrances, and they are a part of every person's struggle toward success and destiny. Failure, however, only comes when one quits or accepts defeat.

Did I learn from my setbacks? I believe that in every setback or negative situation there is a seed of equivalent or greater benefit. The Bible declares firmly:

Romans 8:28, KJV

And we know that all things work together for good to them that love God, to them who are the called according to his purpose.

At my very worst moments, if I have the right attitude and perspective, I can make lemons into lemonade. It's all about how I perceive a thing and how I react to it and whether I learn from it and grow from it or not.

Perseverance is one of the essential elements you can find in every successful individual. What is perseverance? It is pressing through, continuing to go forward. It's about getting up and going back in the ring. It's not about how many times you get knocked down, but how many times you get back up.

This was true of the great Abraham Lincoln and of so many other great leaders, who overcame great hardships. Think of men like Theodore Roosevelt, Franklin Roosevelt and Thomas Edison.

Do I have a winning attitude? Do I have an attitude of compassion? Do I have an attitude of commitment? Do I have an attitude that is open to cooperation? Am I a person who has a tendency to get into a clique? If I want a team spirit and cooperation, I have to know that I can't participate in (and certainly can't initiate) back-biting of a fellow believer, pitting one against another, cliques and/or an elitist attitude.

In a positive mode of leadership, I must remain upbeat and be ready to take advantage of every opportunity that presents itself. I have to be affirming and encouraging of others without crossing the line into using flattery to manipulate or control others. Compliments without truth or sincerity can cause more harm than good.

People know when you're being truthful. I need to have a healthy self-image and not continually require affirmation from someone else in order to be happy with my life or myself. If not, I will be basically codependent. Like David, sooner or later we have to encourage ourselves in the Lord (see 1 Samuel 30:6).

I have to understand that my place of blessing is in my covenant with God and that my covenant position is sure:

Deuteronomy 8:18, KJV

> *But thou shalt remember the LORD thy God: for it is he that giveth thee power to get wealth, that he may establish his covenant which he sware unto thy fathers, as it is this day.*

I can do great and mighty exploits, just as Daniel declared:

Daniel 11:32, KJV

> *But the people that do know their God shall be strong, and do exploits.*

I have to know that happiness is a choice, much more of a decision than an emotion. I have to stop worrying about the things I can't change. I have to learn to be content with who I am, knowing that

God makes all things good and He puts everything I need in me to succeed.

An important part of leadership is striving for excellence. Committing myself to excellence means doing the very best I can do, not compromising my integrity for short-term gain, but basing my life on the moral, ethical and biblical values that Christ has laid out for us.

I need to be a person of enthusiasm, for enthusiasm is contagious. If I am going to successfully lead, there are certain things that I am going to have to develop within myself: enthusiasm, perseverance and a positive mental attitude. These are all intertwined. It's all about living life from the inside out. It's about being honest with myself, about how I'm thinking, how I'm acting and how I'm reacting.

LET US PURSUE EXCELLENCE

So, let us aim high. The goal is excellence, an excellent spirit, an excellent anointing to lead. Once you catch a vision from the Lord for your life, you then know your potential. Press toward it every single day. We must give up our small ambitions and know that we were created for something much greater.

Paul wrote to the Philippian believers:

Philippians 1:10, KJV

That ye may approve things that are excellent; that ye may be sincere and without offence till the day of Christ.

Not only should we pursue excellence, but at all costs, we need to avoid offence. The spirit of offence is the first thing that will take you out of your ministry—if you allow it to land near you in any way.

Set goals and time limits on those goals. Don't procrastinate. Do something to be active in achieving those goals.

Philippians 3:13-14, KJV

Brethren, I count not myself to have apprehended: but this one thing I do, forgetting those things which are behind, and reaching forth unto those things which are before, I press toward the mark for the prize of the high calling of God in Christ Jesus.

Maintain a positive attitude and stay around positive people. Stay focused on your objective, not your obstacles. Don't look back, but ahead. Don't give up. Don't quit! That is the only way a Christian can lose!

If you will press toward these goals, the spirit of a

leader will rest on your soul, and you will find many gathering around you.

> **Lord, I pray that the spirit of the leader would rise up within us in a stronger way, in a new way, in a bold way. As we cry out, like Solomon, for the wisdom of a leader, I pray that we will have understanding of the visionary realm, the realm of the fore-runner, the realm of knowing we can do all things through Christ that strengthens us.**
>
> **Father, You know the right time for every leader reading this book to begin to gather others to themselves. I pray, Lord, that we will not go before You, but that we will learn to wait upon You as You renew our strength.**
>
> **I pray also, Lord, that we move out, advancing the Kingdom, knowing who we are in You and the authority we possess.**
>
> **In Jesus' name,**
> **Amen!**

IF WE RUN AWAY FROM THE CHURCH, WE WILL FIND OURSELVES RUNNING AWAY FROM OUR GIFTING, OUR CALLING, OUR VERY DESTINY!

Chapter 11

Knowing and Understanding the Visionary Realm

Proverbs 29:18, KJV

Where there is no vision, the people perish: but he that keepeth the law, happy is he.

Now let's talk about vision. You can't talk about leadership without fully coming to an understanding of the visionary realm.

The visionary realm is a realm of the prophetic and one of the ways the Lord uses to speak to His people. Proverbs 29:18 is a spiritual truth that is so important we might call it a spiritual law. As noted, just as natural laws (such as Gravity, Inertia and Relativity) govern the natural realm, spiritual laws govern the spiritual realm. Our ignorance or indifference to either a natural or spiritual law doesn't change the fact that there is a cause and effect. If we do not adhere to that law, we will suffer the consequences.

I am a simple person and when I heard this scripture first spoken in church, I was disappointed. I didn't have a vision and didn't understand vision. So, according to this law, I was doomed to perish — if this was, in fact, a spiritual truth.

Proverbs are spiritual laws that can affect our lives in a practical way. The Bible is a guide to successful Christian living, and Proverbs give us a practical view of how to apply these principles to our lives. It is absolutely essential that we have an understanding of vision and the visionary realm if we are to successfully lead God's people forward.

We need to know how to catch a vision, how to cast a vision and how to run with a vision. We need to know the difference between a personal vision, a corporate vision and a Kingdom vision. We also need to be able to spiritually discern between the vision of God and the vision of man.

One of the fastest ways to find yourself lost is by following someone who is going to a different destination. It is so easy to be distracted or even deceived.

When God's vision is revealed, His sheep hear His voice. Those with a like spirit and like heart get a witness in their spirit. This witness confirms God's

Word. When the corporate or Kingdom vision of God is revealed or cast, those of like heart will find their place and their part in the vision. The personal vision that is revealed for each of us should show us how the various parts of the Body of Christ are to fit together for the fulfillment of the corporate vision.

The vision of God reveals His heart, His purpose of God, and the vision of man reveals the heart or purpose of man in a particular situation. When people gather around the vision of God, they gather around the heart and purpose of God for that area, season, city, etc. When we gather around the vision of man, we are not gathering around God, but around man.

Man's time is measured in minutes, but God's time is measured in eternity. His purposes are not carnal in nature, but spiritual. The same cannot be said for man. A prophetic people, a prophetic generation, will not only hear the voice of God, but will also respond and capture the vision. Then they will run with the vision.

Since God is not only the Author of our faith, but also the Finisher of our faith and Jehovah Jireh, our Provider, He will bring together all the parts, pieces, people and resources necessary, not just to birth, but also to build, sustain and maintain His vision.

What has happened in Eagle Worldwide Ministries in nearly twenty years has very little to do with any one man or woman. In fact, most of the things that God has done through us have been accomplished when I was nowhere around. It happened because the vision was not of man, but of God.

The works done through this ministry are examples of what can happen when there is a vision: the birthing of our individual churches, the birthing of our Retreat & Revival Centre, our Summer Camp, our intern program, the King's Way Outreach Centre, our various outreach ministries, our Centre for Excellence and Gage Park Outreaches, our missionary travel team and our Network of Ministers and Ministries.

God has sent us men and women of like heart and like spirit, those who have captured the vision of God and are able to fulfill a portion of their personal vision and mission in life through the corporate and Kingdom vision. This is all part of God's plan for multiplication and duplication.

And God has a plan for the end-time harvest. Most men dream big dreams, but a few actually wake up and make their dreams become reality. This usually comes from the understanding and the relationship they have with God and their application of the vision of God with the resources He provides. First, you have your mission. Then, you develop a strategy. And, finally, you must have a plan of action.

It is by active faith that we give our vision wings. It is by the unity of the Spirit and cooperating together in that Spirit of unity that we can bring forth the commanded blessing of God.

The psalmist declared:

Psalm 133:1-3, KJV

Behold, how good and how pleasant it is for brethren to dwell together in unity! It is like the precious ointment upon the head, that ran down upon the beard, even Aaron's beard: that went down to the skirts of his garments; as the dew of Hermon, and as the dew that descended upon the mountains of Zion: for there the LORD *commanded the blessing, even life for evermore.*

This type of unity comes only as we learn how to pray together, how to plan together, and how to work together, and this is clearly God's will for our lives today. As we have seen, Jesus said so in His wonderful prayer:

John 17:21, KJV

That they all may be one; as thou, Father, art in me, and I in thee, that they also may be one

in us: that the world may believe that thou hast
sent me.

When we get distracted, discouraged, divided
or in some point of disunity (by our own personal
initiative, ambition or pride), we are not necessarily
under a curse, because Christ took the curse of the
Law upon Himself:

Galatians 3:13, KJV
Christ hath redeemed us from the curse of the
law, being made a curse for us: for it is written,
cursed is every one that hangeth on a tree.

However, the blessing of God and the anointing
of God is obviously not there. What we must do is
recapture the vision and blessing of God and not the
vision of man. Let's unite again around God's vision.

There are a lot of good things to do, but we need to do
the "God thing." We need to capture the vision, understand the mission, develop a strategy and write out an
action plan. Then, according to Habakkuk 2:1-5, we need
to run with the vision in a spirit of unity and harmony.

Following God is not complicated. It's not necessarily easy, but it is also not complicated. It is the
thoughts and the mind of man that complicate the

simplicity of the heart and purpose of God. God is not hard to catch, nor is His vision. He is not running away from us. He wants to be found by us, so let us chase after Him, not after man!

Let us capture the vision of God and then let's run with it.

VISION QUEST

A vision is a thought, you see,
In your mind's eye, that sets you free.
It is a dream that you hold dear.
And, in your heart, it's always near.

It can be strong or bold, you know,
A thought that sets your heart aglow.
It can be kind and gentle things,
That give your heart and soul their wings.

It's thoughts of all that you can be
If only there for you to see.
I have a goal. Thank God for that.
On something real I hang my hat.

I believe in things unseen,
My faith sustaining me in between.

I pray you rise above the rest
And reach your dream,
Your vision quest!

YOUR PERSONAL VISION

Now, let's talk about your personal vision. The Lord has a plan for your life. Jeremiah spoke for the Lord when he said:

Jeremiah 29:11-13, KJV

For I know the thoughts that I think toward you, saith the LORD, thoughts of peace, and not of evil, to give you an expected end. Then shall ye call upon me, and ye shall go and pray unto me, and I will hearken unto you. And ye shall seek me, and find me, when ye shall search for me with all your heart.

This scripture is not just an evangelistic tool; it is a solid truth from the Word of God. God has a plan for each of us, and it is our responsibility to seek Him so that we can find that plan.

In the same way, Habakkuk sought the Lord:

Habakkuk 2:1-4, KJV

> *I will stand upon my watch, and set me upon the tower, and will watch to see what he will say unto me, and what I shall answer when I am reproved. And the LORD answered me, and said, write the vision, and make it plain upon tables, that he may run that readeth it. For the vision is yet for an appointed time, but at the end it shall speak, and not lie: though it tarry, wait for it; because it will surely come, it will not tarry. Behold, his soul which is lifted up is not upright in him: but the just shall live by his faith.*

You and I must keep track of what the Lord speaks to us, for His desire is to share with us His vision and purpose for our lives. Then we must have wisdom to know the timing of the vision. And, finally, we must have the patience necessary to wait for the vision and the perseverance to walk it out in our daily lives.

Proverbs declares:

Proverbs 16:3, KJV

> *Commit thy works unto the LORD, and thy thoughts shall be established.*

In addition to having a full understanding of God's vision and purpose for ourselves (which is a life-time goal), we must establish other goals that can serve as stepping stones and sign posts in the pursuit of our ultimate purpose.

The fulfillment and achievement of the short-term goals help us, not only to build character, but they also encourage us and build our self-esteem and our understanding that with God we can achieve all things. Faith to live by is the reality of our daily Christian life and the reality of that message.

A man without a vision is like a ship without a rudder. We must be people who are achievement oriented, which is to expect fruit from the work God has called us to. The apostolic prayer that Paul prayed, as recorded in Ephesians, asked the Lord to give us a Spirit of wisdom and revelation and understanding, so that we would know the hope of our calling. This is our purpose in life:

Ephesians 1:17-19, KJV

> *That the God of our Lord Jesus Christ, the Father of glory, may give unto you the spirit of wisdom and revelation in the knowledge of him: the eyes of your understanding being enlightened; that ye may know what is the hope*

of his calling, and what the riches of the glory of his inheritance in the saints, and what is the exceeding greatness of his power to us-ward who believe, according to the working of his mighty power.

Paul also wrote to the Colossians that God wanted us to be filled with the knowledge of His will:

Colossians 1:9-10, KJV

For this cause we also, since the day we heard it, do not cease to pray for you, and to desire that ye might be filled with the knowledge of his will in all wisdom and spiritual understanding; that ye might walk worthy of the Lord unto all pleasing, being fruitful in every good work, and increasing in the knowledge of God.

This is God's will for each of us. And what is it again? That we would walk worthy of our calling and that we would be fruitful. In other words, be men and women of accomplishment in every good works. God's desire is that we are fruitful for His Kingdom, so that we bring glory to His name.

The writer of Hebrews showed that God wants to make us perfect in every good work so that we can do His will (see Hebrews 13:21). In addition to these goals being stepping stones to our purpose and signposts to keep us on track, they help to encourage and challenge us. They help to direct our decisions, thoughts and energy and redirect us when we get off track. In this way, we can avoid frustrations:

Proverbs 13:20, KJV

> *He that walketh with wise men shall be wise; but a companion of fools shall be destroyed."*

Jeremiah 1:4-5, KJV

> *Then the Word of the Lord came unto me, saying, before I formed thee in the belly I knew thee; and before thou camest forth out of the womb I sanctified thee, and I ordained thee a prophet unto the nations.*

1 Timothy 4:12, KJV

> *Let no man despise thy youth; but be thou an example of the believers, in word, in conversation, in charity, in spirit, in faith, in purity.*

Philippians 3:14, KJV

> *I press toward the mark for the prize of the high calling of God in Christ Jesus.*

Many people pursue some call of God but don't understand His "high" call. They settle for doing any needed thing or get distracted by the good. Sometimes, however, a good thing can actually keep us from the God thing. We must each seek the "high" call of God for our lives and then stay focused on it. Some obviously don't know the purposes of God or are not yet willing to pay the price to see those purposes fulfilled.

Here is the progression of your vision:

THE PROGRESSION OF YOUR VISION

1. Receiving the Revelation
2. Understanding the Vision or Purpose
3. Establishing Goals
4. Developing a Strategy
5. Preparing a Plan of Action

All men dream big dreams, but those who become fruitful and successful wake up and make their dreams become reality.

Father, this day I pray to have a deeper understanding of the visionary realm. Lord, teach me to catch a vision from You, to cast

a vision and to run with a vision. I pray, Lord, that my vision will be Your vision, and I will see with Your eyes further than I have ever seen before. Open the eyes of my understanding, Lord.

As a prophetic person, Lord, part of this prophetic generation, I pray to hear Your voice and no other. Lord, I thank You for the vision and plan You have for my life., Your Word says that before You formed me, You ordained me. I pray now, Father, that I would walk in Your wisdom and be fruitful in the hope of Your calling and my purpose.

Lord, I pray for Your wisdom in the strategy I must use to take the appropriate action in establishing the required goals toward fulfilling the revelation of the vision You have given me to fulfill and to live out.

In Jesus' name,

Amen!

WHEN WE LEAVE THIS WORLD, IT WILL BE THE SAME WAY WE CAME INTO IT— NAKED AND VULNERABLE!

Chapter 12

The Importance of Mentoring Prospective Leaders

3 John 4

I have no greater joy than to hear that my children are walking in the truth.

I cannot emphasize enough the importance of discipleship and mentoring. Personally, I believe that this should be a lifestyle for all believers. In this chapter, I will show you why this is so important to the Church today.

We, as seasoned Christians, should always be ready to purpose in ourselves to pour into the next generation. This is what the Christian life is all about. And this is not just for those who are behind the pulpit. It is the responsibility of every person who calls themselves a born-again believer.

Barnabas mentored Paul, and Paul mentored Timothy. Elijah mentored Elisha, and he received a double-portion anointing. As our text verse reveals, John, the disciple of Jesus, also knew the joy of mentoring others.

Let us be those men and women who hear the heart of God in discipleship and reach out to others, pouring into them what God has given to us. Let us be trustworthy, to allow another person to come alongside of us or for us to come alongside of someone we know is on this journey of fulfilling their destiny. Let us be history-makers and world-changers, as we purpose to build a foundation in a generation that God is raising up. Let us get ready and equipped and position ourselves for one of the greatest events that will take place on this planet.

In years past, we visited hundreds of churches, both large and small, and many of the people we met had been in the church now for a very long time. Some have been saved for ten years and others for double that, and yet they have never really been discipled properly or mentored. Some of them suffer or are continually challenged, living on a roller-coaster-like spiritual walk. When we dig a little deeper as to what's causing these peaks and valleys, these ups and downs, the evidence keeps pointing back to a lack of discipleship and mentoring.

As we have seen, discipleship is having the foundational principles of the faith systematically instilled into our lives that will give us a solid understanding of the Word of God, the foundations of our faith and how to apply them practically in our lives in a manner that will bring successful Christian living. It's about the hearts of the fathers being turned to the children and the hearts of the children to the fathers.

Again, mentoring is when the discipleship foundation has been laid in my life, and God sends leaders who see the potential in me and are willing to take the necessary time to identify and hone the gifts, talents and abilities that God has given me and to pour into my life. In a very real sense, they are to build into my life from their own experiences and bring forth the potential that is within me for spiritual and natural success.

I thank God for the men and women He has placed in my life for discipleship and also for mentoring. I thank God for my parents and grandparents, teachers and coaches, who all laid a foundation in my life and taught me life skills. Some of those basic things, which I often take for granted, would not be in my life if it were not for the sacrifice of these people.

There have also been pastors and other spiritual leaders, like Dave Gey, who was the Vice President of my company for many years. Dave was the area leader for the Fellowship of Christian Athletes. I am also indebted to the instructors and staff at the Brownsville Revival School of Ministry. I must always honor the men and women God has put in my life, even though I will only ever worship God Himself.

After that initial foundation was laid, I was ready for God to send mentors into my life, men like Paul Wetzel, of Pensacola, Florida, who was (and still is) my pastor. He taught me a lot about church and church protocol.

There were woman too. Principle among them were Ruth Heflin and Jane Lowder from Calvary Pentecostal Tabernacle and Campground. They mentored me and imparted into me in the area of my prophetic call and modeled for me what it is like to be a prophetic missionary to the nations and how to flow in the Spirit and in my gifting.

There was Joan Gieson, who worked ten years with Benny Hinn and eight years with Kathryn Kuhlman. She was the number two person in the number one healing ministry in the world twice. She had a great hands-on healing anointing on her own life. She was like a spiritual mother to Pastor Mave and me, and she actually introduced us to each other.

We both had worked with Joan and were mentored by her in two different areas of her ministry. She didn't just teach us the methods of how to pray for the sick, but she modeled for us a walk of love and compassion, mixed with an amazing gift of faith. She had faith, not just to heal the sick, but also to believe for the unbelievable. She taught us how to believe in ourselves and the gift and calling of God on our lives.

There were many other people who helped us along the way. I sometimes think back on the times I cried out to God: "When?" "Why?" "How?" "Who?" "What's taking so long?" In the end, I discovered that I was the one who was taking so long. I was in the process of preparing my own heart to be able to learn, to be able to receive. The burden of teaching is on the teacher, but the burden of learning is on the student. When the student is ready, the teacher will appear.

In recent years, God has been taking me back spiritually and naturally to my roots—the Pensacola Revival and Calvary Campground—and has been increasing the anointing on my life in the renewal of these relationships. We have seen an increase of healings and miracles and a prophetic flow that makes me ever so thankful for those who were able to build into me a hunger in my heart for revival and for a fresh move of the Spirit.

Sister Ruth Heflin taught us that the gift of prophecy is the voice of revival. What follows is a prophetic word that she spoke over the state of Alabama in November of 1996. Pastor John Kilpatrick and his people at the Church of His Presence in Daphne, Alabama have been praying and proclaiming this word. Pastor Mave and I visited them in Mobile at the Bay of the Holy Spirit, where they were experiencing a fresh wind of the Spirit. Here is what Ruth prophesied:

> *Come and go with me to Alabama, for I shall make the state a beautiful way. I shall raise her up, and the wind of God shall blow upon her and through her, and the many shall come alive with my life. I, the Lord, shall be a blazing fire running through Alabama.*
>
> *Alabama, know ye this: that even now the winds of God that blow upon thee shall be the power of God that sets many free. For I, the Lord,*

shall run through you. Run with My power, run with My joy, run with strength and bring people out.

They shall come out in the strength and witness of My glory and the blessing and fire of My Spirit, and they will say what they couldn't say before, do what they couldn't do before, and be who they have never been before. They shall be naturally supernatural and work the works of the impossible and turn the heads of the children of men.

Listen to me! Keep your eyes upon Alabama. For I say, "She shall be one that will make the news, and many shall come from far and wide. And they shall come in cars and planes and trains, to see what God is doing."

I say, "She shall be like a banjo upon My knee, and I will play a song on her that shall reach around the world. Come and go with Me and see Alabama set men free."

I am so thankful to God for allowing me to sit under Sister Ruth's ministry and have her as a mentor. God will always send the right person, the right individual, at just the right time to sow into your life. Proverbs states:

Proverbs 17:17

> *A friend loves at all times,*
> *and a brother is born for adversity.*

Whatever the season and whatever the need, the Lord will put the right person in your life. I challenge you today to position yourself and to humble your heart. Let the eyes of your understanding be enlightened, that you may see, hear and know the prophetic time and season for your life. May you also recognize the divine appointments, those golden connections that God has ordained for you for such a time as this!

If you need mentoring, then others do too. Evangelism is about making disciples. So, what is your responsibility in this regard? Often we convince an individual that Jesus is Lord, or the Spirit of the Lord convicts them, and they receive Jesus as their Savior. But that is just the beginning. Them saying the sinner's prayer (which we, in the Church, consider to be a prayer of conversion), is not necessarily the same as having a born-again experience.

A person, any person, is saved by actually believing in their heart that God raised the Lord Jesus Christ from the dead and that He is alive today, receiving Jesus as their personal Savior and then declaring that He is Lord of their life. Them hearing the Gospel is only one part of the process. Our witness and our testimony is another part. Their response is, again, another part. It is not the whole.

When we know that we have given an individual enough information to make a decision, or at other times, when we feel that they have made that decision, we need to mentally, emotionally and naturally walk them through the process of faith, acceptance and declaration. Then they are ready to begin to grow. Far too often those of us who came to know Jesus as Lord through the testimony or ministry or others are left to our own resources to know how to follow Christ.

When we lead someone to the Lord, that's wonderful, but it is just the beginning. Now that they are a believer, it is our responsibility to bring them to real discipleship:

John 8:31-32, NKJV

> *Then Jesus said to those Jews who believed Him, "If you abide in My word, you are My disciples indeed. And you shall know the truth, and the truth shall make you free."*

Sometimes the circumstances around us at the time we lead someone to the reality of Christ dictate very little contact in that individual's future. We need to get whatever information we can so that we can follow up, get them connected to a church and make sure they have access to a Bible. If we know them, and we are disciples ourselves, then it's time to begin to disciple others.

What do we need to do?

1. Get them a Bible.
2. Get their phone number.
3. Begin to form a relationship with them.
4. Find a church in their area that you can recommend and put them in contact with it.
5. Follow up with them regularly.
6. Do as much of the actual discipleship as is possible or practical. This would include teaching them:
   - The fundamental truths of our faith
   - The importance of:
   1. Developing some form of regular Bible study
   2. Finding their place in the life of Body of Christ
   3. Having a prayer life and sufficient fellowship to develop proper relationships

In this way, you are building a spiritual house:

Psalm 127:1-5, KJV

> *Except the LORD build the house, they labour in vain that build it: except the LORD keep the city, the watchman waketh but in vain. It is vain for you to rise up early, to sit up late, to eat the bread of sorrows: for so he giveth his beloved sleep. Lo, children are an heritage of the LORD: and the fruit of the womb is his reward. As arrows are in the hand of a mighty man; so are children of the youth. Happy is the man that hath his quiver full of them: they shall not be ashamed, but they shall speak with the enemies in the gate.*

Sons and daughters are the way the Lord builds His house. The Word declares, concerning having natural children, *"Happy is the man that hath his quiver full of them,"* and a quiver full of arrows enables a man to do some serious warfare.

Aaron's sons were anointed and consecrated. Elisha was the spiritual son of Elijah, and he went on to do greater things than his spiritual father. Elijah had thrown his cloak around Elisha for the symbolic transference of sonship (see 1 Kings 19:19). And God has an Elijah for you today. As Malachi declared:

Malachi 4:5-6, KJV

> *Behold, I will send you Elijah the prophet before the coming of the great and dreadful day of the LORD: and he shall turn the heart of the fathers to the children, and the heart of the children to their fathers, lest I come and smite the earth with a curse.*

This end-time prophet will turn the heart of the fathers to the children and the heart of the children to their fathers.

Incidentally, Elijah was the most successful person in the Old Testament at reproducing himself. He did fourteen miracles, but Elisha did twenty-eight. That's the goal.

I firmly believe that God is awakening in the heart of ministry spiritual fathers who have a desire for the next generation. Many times, in the past, great ministries have ceased at the death or retirement of the founding minister. When we don't impart to others, there is a breach of power or a lack of increase in ministry, and it eventually dies.

When God created the world, He created man with a seed inside of him (see Genesis 1:11). God could have created an entire world full of inhabitants, but His plan was for us to give us the privilege of bringing forth sons and daughters. He created the apostolic and prophetic ministries with the ability to reproduce themselves through impartation to spiritual sons and daughters.

As we have seen, Paul wrote:

1 Corinthians 4:15, KJV

For though ye have ten thousand instructors in Christ, yet have ye not many fathers: for in Christ Jesus I have begotten you through the gospel.

When someone teaches you something, you receive information and grow, but when someone has fathered you in the Spirit, you receive an impartation of their anointing. In the apostolic, there is the ability to birth other ministers, but also to impart and empower them in a unique way. Paul's ministry not only increased; it multiplied through his sons and daughters.

Today, wherever I happen to be physically, I have sons and daughters who are faithfully working on our campground, in our King's Way Ministry, in our office and as pastors and elders in our churches. This didn't just happen. I had to plant the seeds for it and then disciple and train our leaders one by one.

Criteria for Discipling

There are different levels and degrees of discipleship and mentoring. We, as Christians, must always be ready and have a hunger to win souls. There are, however, many who are simply not prepared to disciple others. Perhaps they are not very strong or secure in their own walk of faith with Christ. Perhaps they are not as intelligent or understanding or the other person may already be further along in their walk than they are. They may not have enough in common with that individual to mentor them. In such a case, we need to have the wisdom and humility to make the right recommendation to that person in need of discipleship, concerning the right individual or church or fellowship that can be of help to them.

When I choose to disciple someone, whether it is in a group setting or on an individual basis, it is always a personal thing, and that requires relationship, time and taking responsibility. I have to know in my heart that this is a responsibility God Himself has given me because this person I am to disciple is special and unique to God, and therefore I can never take that responsibility lightly.

If I choose to do this, then I have chosen to be dependable, organized and disciplined, because discipling requires much teaching. I also have to know and sense when my efforts at discipleship are not working and be willing to change my plan and alter my course in order to help that individual.

Father, You are so awesome and so faithful. I pray for the Spirit of Wisdom and Counsel, that as we reach out and disciple and mentor those You would bring into our lives, they would see Jesus in us. May we exercise the fruits of the Spirit and be quick to listen and slow to speak. May we help to facilitate the shaping and sharpening of a generation that is coming up behind us.

I pray, Lord, that they would be enabled by Your Spirit to surpass that which we have even dreamed of and to accomplish great things for Your glory. Thank You, Lord.

In Jesus' name,
Amen!

TRUE MEEKNESS COMES IN UNDERSTANDING THE VALUE OF SUBMITTING TO AUTHORITY THE SAME WAY A THOROUGHBRED SUBMITS TO ITS RIDER!

Chapter 13

The Spiritual Progression in Effective Leadership

Ephesians 1:17-18, KJV

> *That the God of our Lord Jesus Christ, the Father of glory, may give unto you the spirit of wisdom and revelation in the knowledge of him: the eyes of your understanding being enlightened; that ye may know what is the hope of his calling, and what the riches of the glory of his inheritance in the saints.*

It is a time to pour into a new generation that is rising up to walk in power and authority, a generation that encompasses a range of ages, from the very young to even the strongly mature. I believe it is time for spiritual fathers and mothers to rise up and impart the vast treasures of knowledge and experience they have gained as they have traveled in this walk with our Lord.

As noted, you cannot lead someone where you have never been, but wherever you are in your journey with the Lord right now and with all that you have been through, know that God has been preparing you *"for such a time as this."*

In this chapter, I want to outline for you your prophetic journey. You were formed for a purpose, for a destiny, which the Bible tells us existed before the foundations of the world, and you need to stay true to that purpose. God is revealing and releasing His people, His Church. We can lead and pour into a new generation when we know that we have traveled that road and experienced what works.

Let's all help raise up this next generation, a generation that has been fatherless and motherless. Let us nurture them and be there for them. Let us speak into their lives and breathe life into them with the power of our words and the role model of our faith.

Prophetically, in this current season, we are standing at the threshold of the greatest harvest ever known to man and also the greatest battle. These are the days of the harvest. These are the days of Elijah. The fields are white and ready for the reapers. Let us go forth to reap.

Malachi 3 and 4 clearly speak of the season we are in. This is the time when the messenger is sent with purifying fire, to purge away that which is not of the Spirit, so that the gold and the silver will remain in our lives.

Each of us is at a different place spiritually in our journey, and sometimes we have a difficult time identifying our destiny call. Our text verse for this chapter is the great apostolic prayer of Paul. We need to realize that the Lord wants us to be both spiritually and naturally successful, not one or the other. He wants to prosper us even as our souls prosper.

God's Word shows us that it would do you no good at all to *"gain the whole world and lose* [your] *soul"*:

Matthew 16:26, KJV

> *For what is a man profited, if he shall gain the whole world, and lose his own soul? or what shall a man give in exchange for his soul?*

Having natural, personal financial success without the accompanying spiritual success leaves a person empty. Success is not the destination but, rather, the journey. I need to clearly know where I am going, but I also need to rightly identify who I am in Christ and where I am in this journey.

I believe that there are five cycles, or passages, to our spiritual destiny and many different phases within those passages. The five passages I speak of are as follows:

- DISCIPLESHIP
- MENTORING
- ACHIEVEMENT
- LEADERSHIP
- LEGACY

THE DIFFERENCE BETWEEN DISCIPLESHIP AND MENTORING

These are two different roles and functions altogether. As I am sure you are aware, in the natural, we are a fatherless generation, a "parentless" generation. As it is in the natural, so it is in the Spirit. For the most part, there is a lack of real discipleship in the Church today. Discipleship has become a lost art. Many of us were birthed into the Kingdom in some evangelistic way, but no one ever really discipled us. As noted, the Great Commission is not to make converts, but to *make disciples.* Discipleship is a form of shepherding.

Shepherding, or discipleship, is pastoral in nature. It includes setting the foundations of relationships in place in an individual's life. It is placement in relationship to the rest of the Body. It is for person, home, church, family and career, and it's a time of laying a foundation in each believer for a successful Christian life.

Discipleship encompasses counseling, visitation and relationship. It is gaining a foundational understanding of the Word, the cross, the blood, the armor of God and how to apply the Word of God to my life, so that I can live successfully in this world. It's all about the victorious life.

Many people want to become leaders, but in the Kingdom of God, before you can become a leader, you must first be a good disciple. Some people come to me, looking to be mentored as leaders, but they are not yet even good disciples. We have to first become a disciple before we can become a leader. I send them back to their pastor, to their shepherd, to get a more sure foundation on which to build a spiritual future.

As noted, the prophet Malachi declared:

Malachi 4:6, KJV

And he shall turn the heart of the fathers to the children, and the heart of the children to their fathers, lest I come and smite the earth with a curse.

What is true discipleship? It's like David sang in Psalm 34:

Psalm 34:8, KJV

O taste and see that the LORD is good.

I have tasted and found that the Lord is good. Therefore, I now testify that the Lord is good and welcome others to join me in tasting of Him. That is discipleship.

Proverbs 1-9 contains Solomon's written advice to his son, Rehoboam. Rehoboam later became king himself:

2 Chronicles 10:1, KJV

And Rehoboam went to Shechem: for to Shechem were all Israel come to make him king.

All of us need counsel and wisdom, as noted:

Proverbs 4:7, KJV

Wisdom is the principal thing; therefore get wisdom and with all thy getting get understanding.

1 Corinthians 3:18-19, KJV

> *Let no one deceive himself. If anyone among you seems to be wise in this age, let him become a fool that he may become wise. For the wisdom of this world is foolishness with God. For it is written, He taketh the wise in their own craftiness.*

The question is: where should we look for wise counsel? Each of us, in any particular stage of life, needs the wisdom that comes through counseling with others. This counseling is normally done with older, more experienced people. Rehoboam, when he began his reign, sought such counsel:

2 Chronicles 10:6-7

> *Then King Rehoboam consulted the elders who had served his father Solomon during his lifetime. "How would you advise me to answer these people?" he asked. They replied, "If you will be kind to these people and please them and give them a favorable answer, they will always be your servants."*

Sadly, however, Rehoboam rejected the counsel of the elders and, instead, sought the advice of immature people:

2 Chronicles 10:8-10, CSB

> *But he rejected the advice of the elders who had advised him, and he consulted with the young men who had grown up with him, the ones attending him. He asked them, "What message do you advise we send back to this people who said to me, 'Lighten the yoke your father put on us?'"*
>
> *Then the young men who had grown up with him told him, "This is what you should say to the people who said to you, 'Your father made our yoke heavy, but you, make it lighter on us!' This is what you should say to them: 'My little finger is thicker than my father's waist!'"*

Obviously, the younger men Rehoboam took counsel from lacked experience and wisdom. And he suffered because of it.

We all need godly, not ungodly counsel:

Psalm 1:1-3, NKJV

> *Blessed is the man*
> *Who walks not in the counsel of the ungodly,*
> *Nor stands in the path of sinners,*
> *Nor sits in the seat of the scornful;*

*But his delight is in the law of the L*ORD,
And in His law he meditates day and night.
He shall be like a tree
Planted by the rivers of water,
That brings forth its fruit in its season,
Whose leaf also shall not wither;
And whatever he does shall prosper.

Rehoboam needed mentoring.

WHAT DO I MEAN BY MENTORING?

This is that stage in our spiritual growth and development in which we are already walking as good disciples with the Lord and are ready to progress to a place where we are equipped and empowered. Mentoring is a time of honing our gifts, talents and abilities, to prepare us for a work of service to the Lord. It is that area of our life where we are now truly the chosen. We have made a choice to begin to extend and advance the Kingdom of God by the work of service in our lives.

Mentoring can be done by a pastor, but normally needs to be done by someone in leadership who is like a life coach already. Why do I say this? Because you can only teach what you know. You can only take me where you have been. In the end, we all bear fruit after our kind. Mentoring must be done by a qualified person.

When God sent me to Calvary Pentecostal Camp, to sit under the ministry of Ruth Heflin, it wasn't to prepare me to live a successful Christian life, but rather, to prepare me for a work of service to the Lord. He sent me there to understand my prophetic gift and my missionary call to the nations.

What does the life of an itinerant minister look like? In all likelihood, I would not have been able to learn in a practical way from someone who had never experienced this or had a working knowledge of it. I needed someone who had lived it and could impart it and cultivate it in my life.

Mentoring is like coaching the individual in their gift, calling, career, life, wealth or destiny. According to *Webster's Dictionary*, a coach is:

One who instructs in the fundamentals.
Directs team strategy
Tutors ... primes with facts ... .
Trains for the race.

That's right, a coach "trains for the race," trains his students, or "mentees," to successfully run the race ahead of them. This is just as valid in the spiritual as it is in the natural:

Isaiah 30:20-21

> *Although the* Lord *gives you the bread of adversity and the water of affliction, your teachers will be hidden no more; with your own eyes you will see them. Whether you turn to the right or to the left, your ears will hear a voice behind you, saying, "This is the way; walk in it."*

It's not about the right or the left, but about the voice behind you. Other people God places in your life can help you through their voice of experience. Consider Moses and Joshua, Elijah and Elisha, Jesus and His disciples (see especially Luke 9 and 10). Winston Churchill once said, "The further back you look, the further ahead you can see." Don't ignore the wise counsel of those around you.

This brings you to achievement.

What Do I Mean By Achievement?

This particular passage of your journey has to do specifically with putting your skills, giftings, talents, abilities and potential into operation and producing results. The heart of the man at the achievement level is at personal peak performance. This is the season when the rubber meets the road. This is the time to implement, activate, focus and function.

At this level, a man or woman has difficulty allowing others to do the work because, obviously, no one can do it as well. They are totally honed in on their target. Production and fruitfulness blind their thoughts, at times, to the future. They are taking their vision and provision and fully producing tangible results with them.

Thus far in their walk, this is the most rewarding season. The strength of the horse within them is fully running the race. They can finally feel the wind blowing in their face, and they feel like this is it. The achiever is finally doing what he or she was born for.

There is absolutely nothing wrong with this stage. It is a necessary season for each of our lives and the life of every leader.

Some people come into the Kingdom from another area of life and immediately want to move into leadership, never having been discipled or properly mentored and having no spiritual achievement, no depth and no maturity. And yet they wonder why no one wants to follow them. It is because they have nothing tangible to show that they have produced. Their teaching is always, "Do as I say, not as I do."

If someone skips the achievement level and moves right into leadership, they will never really be able to have empathy for the person who stumbles and falls and struggles. The best they can hope for is to sympathize with such individuals. A leader needs to fully understand what others are going through. Then you can give them a hand up, not a hand down.

Finally, at this level, the achiever thinks, "Wow, I've arrived!" But we all know that is not the case. This is not the destination, just a whistle stop along the way. The next phase is leadership. God has destined that we be the head and not the tail. We are not on a solo mission. We are part of a great Body, and every member of that Body is to work together toward Kingdom goals. As a leader, we will facilitate this process.

WHAT DO I MEAN BY LEADERSHIP?

With those at the leadership level, suddenly the achiever (or overachiever) has finally reached his or her personal goals, and now their heart turns to multiplication and duplication, because they have come to the reality that they are producing all they can from their own efforts. In order to be more productive, they must now step into a place of management and leadership.

To this point, they've had no problem managing themselves and have proved that with actual achievements. Now, however, they have to refocus their energies toward equipping and empowering others. The focus is no longer on how well they can do a thing, but how well they can teach and coach others to do it.

At the leadership level, a person begins to mentor others in their gifting and calling. The purpose of the five-fold leader in the Church, described so well in Ephesians 4:11-12, is to perfect the saints, to do the work of the ministry, for the edification of the Body of Christ. At the achievement level, people are so focused on their own results that they have no time left or even a desire to sow into the next generation. This level requires completely different personality skills, motivational skills and conflict resolution skills, because it is about preparing, perfecting, equipping and motivating others toward *their* peak performance.

Now the goal is no longer what *I* can do, but what *we* can all do together. It is no longer about *my* vision, but about *our* vision. There is now a great turn in the heart of a man or woman, from the heart of the lion and ministry of the ox, to the heart of the father and the vision of the eagle, seeing the potential in others and deriving personal satisfaction from the achievement of others rather than ourselves.

In this phase of my personal journey, I must instruct others, and here is the progression of my actions:

- First, I do and you watch.
- Next, we do it together.
- Finally, you do it and I watch.

Many times the best leaders, the best coaches, are not always the highest achievers. This level requires a person who has the patience to joyfully walk with and work with others.

Finally, there is legacy.

WHAT DO I MEAN BY LEGACY?

Legacy, at first sight and sound, appears to be secular in nature, but it is actually biblical and spiritual. The promise and the goal is that we will produce fruit, and it will be fruit that lasts.

The Spiritual Progression in Effective Leadership

At the legacy level, we are at a time of transition, a time of great change. It is a time for passing the baton. It is a releasing of those we have trained into their destiny. It is supporting others in their vision. It is the extension and advancement of the Kingdom vision we see in others, enlarging their vision and ministry.

The transition involves reaching back and bringing your experience and life skills to bear on future generations. It is delegating and then releasing others into their destiny call. This is a season of delegation, delegation and more delegation.

At the leadership level, we lead. At the legacy level, we guide. The ball is now in the court of a new generation. They do all the doing, and I do all the watching, while encouraging and guiding, as necessary.

The hardest season for a man or woman of achievement is the season in which they have to sit on the sidelines and watch others pursue their destiny. Within the heart of the father, the heart of the leader, the most wonderful moment of all is when we see our spiritual and natural sons and daughters becoming who they are called to be and reaching their spiritual and natural success and destiny. The greatest gift that we can desire, have or give is to be the man or woman our parents never were, so that our children can be the people we will never be.

Some progress from discipleship to mentoring, to achievement, to leadership and then to legacy. What a wonderful journey!

I hope that through this teaching you are able to discover where you are in your personal prophetic journey of destiny. As I noted at he outset, there are different phases of your journey even within these major passages I have described, when you are transitioning in, when you have settled in and when you are transitioning out into the next new season. I want you to find yourself somewhere in there.

If you are in a place of leadership, may your actions truly be those of a leader and not of a mere achiever. If you are at that season of your life in discipleship, be careful that you are not trying to lead others. This is your season to sit under the heart, life and ministry of another. Your time will come.

As noted, when a student is ready, a teacher will appear. I am believing with you for all of God's blessing, for His right timing and for His perfect guidance. Let His will be done, His Kingdom come in your life and mine.

Lord, I pray that spiritual fathers and mothers would rise up and that we would have a legacy to impart to a new genera-

tion—just as those who have gone before us and pioneered the way for us. Father, I pray for the hearts of the fathers to return to the children, and, Lord, I pray that everyone would understand what season they are in.

I pray for an impartation of wisdom, revelation, leadership and accountability. Teach us, Lord, to see the destinies of those to whom we will pass the baton, that they may continue to run this race with a foundational understanding of discipleship.

In Jesus' name,
Amen!

THERE IS A PLACE BEYOND OBEDIENCE WHERE A PERSON KNOWS WHAT TO DO AND WHEN TO DO IT, AND THEY DO IT BEFORE THEY ARE EVEN ASKED!

Chapter 14

Everything Nice Has a Price

2 Timothy 3:9-17

*But they will not get very far because, as in
the case of those men, their folly will be clear
to everyone. You, however, know all about my
teaching, my way of life, my purpose, faith,
patience, love, endurance, persecutions, suffer-
ings—what kinds of things happened to me in
Antioch, Iconium and Lystra, the persecutions
I endured. Yet the Lord rescued me from all of
them.*

*In fact, everyone who wants to live a godly
life in Christ Jesus will be persecuted, while
evildoers and impostors will go from bad to
worse, deceiving and being deceived. But as
for you, continue in what you have learned and
have become convinced of, because you know*

those from whom you learned it, and how from infancy you have known the Holy Scriptures, which are able to make you wise for salvation through faith in Christ Jesus.

All Scripture is God-breathed and is useful for teaching, rebuking, correcting and training in righteousness, so that the servant of God may be thoroughly equipped for every good work.

Before we build a house, the Lord tells us to count the cost. There is no such thing as a free lunch.

In every career, at least in most, there are occupational hazards. There are some things that you just cannot predict, and many things you cannot prevent. In ministry and in your Christian life and walk, the Word of God tells us that there will be persecution, adversity and division. This is especially true with those in leadership and pioneering.

There will be many ruptures of relationship. Partnerships break up, divorce happens and key people in your life leave or die. There is no natural protection against this. There may also be rebellion, betrayal, disloyalty or infidelity. Just as one of Jesus' twelve disciples betrayed Him, someone in your ministry might well betray you. This hurts, and it hurts bad, but we cannot allow it to keep us from pursuing our dreams and our destiny.

The greater evil would be for me to allow the fear of taking a risk to keep me from God's best. I must know in my heart what it takes, what God expects of me and what it is I'm willing to give, and I must know it even before I begin.

I cannot move forward without faith. As we have seen, Hebrews 11:6 declares, *"Without faith it is impossible to please God."* And, as I mentioned in an earlier chapter, we must focus on the vision:

Luke 9:62, NKJV

> *But Jesus said to him, "No one, having put his hand to the plow, and looking back, is fit for the Kingdom of God."*

As we function in that vision, we must maintain our faith because, *"Faith without works is dead"* (James 2:26).

Wherever I go, I am continually asked to provide mentoring to business leaders, ministers, Bible school graduates, deacons and elders. As we have seen, Paul wrote:

1 Corinthians 4:15

> *For though you might have ten thousand instructors in Christ, yet you do not have many*

fathers; for in Christ Jesus I have begotten you through the gospel.

I will never apologize for pouring into those who are ready to give of themselves. In fact, I am looking for them so that I can pour into them. These are vessels that will hold the blessing when it comes to leadership and raising up leaders.

God is looking for someone who will not quit, someone who will not give up. The following poem by an anonymous author clearly defines that person who will not give up and not give in, a person who has the heart of a leader, the heart of a winner, the heart that will not quit.

Don't Quit

When things go wrong, as they sometimes will,
When the road you're trudging seems all uphill,
When the funds are low and the debts are high,
And you want to smile, but you have to sigh,

When care is pressing you down a bit,
Rest, if you must, but don't you quit.
Life is queer with its twists and turns,
As every one of us sometimes learns.

Everything Nice Has a Price

And many a failure turns about,
When he might have won had he stuck it out.
Don't give up though the pace seems slow.
You may succeed with another blow.

Often the goal is nearer than
It seems to a faint and faltering man,
Often the struggler has given up,
When he might have captured the victor's cup.

And he learned too late when the night slipped
down,
How close he was to the golden crown.
Success is failure turned inside out,
The silver tint of the clouds of doubt.

And you never can tell how close you are.
It may be near when it seems so far.
So stick to the fight when you're hardest hit—
It's when things seem worst that you MUST
NOT QUIT.

It all comes down to attitude. If you think you're beaten you are (please see my poem in a previous chapter). It all depends on your willing mindset. Who would be willing to follow a man or woman whose attitude is beaten before they have even started? People want to follow someone with a heart and an attitude to win.

In the end, we have talked about leadership styles in this book and you have heard my heart. We have talked about the mechanics of leadership. We have talked about the importance of certain skills and character traits. We have talked about the journey and the process. We have talked about the vision and focus. We have talked about goal setting. We have talked about multiplication and duplication and we have talked about the spirit of leadership, the anointing to lead.

Finally, sooner or later we have to get to where the rubber meets the road. Sooner or later we have to get up and start doing it. We have to answer the call. We have to respond to the challenge. The fastest horse doesn't always win the race. Stick in there. Even though everything that is nice has a price, in God's Kingdom the result is worth whatever price we have to pay.

I want to challenge you today to pursue a successful life with all the zeal and all the passion, faith and hope you can muster. There is an emptiness in the performance and function of a leader who has no cause and who has no quest.

Get moving, and be ready pay whatever price is required.

> **Father, I pray for myself and all who read this book that we would walk in the faith that pleases You, faith that requires the action of a true leader. I pray that the vision You have given would be always before us and that we would be faithful to the task at hand. I pray that You would give each person Your supernatural energy to accomplish their destinies and those whom You would bring to walk alongside of them, for the many and different seasons of their walk.**
>
> **Lord, may every situation of our lives be God-used and Father-filtered. May the thought of giving up never be an option for us. Instead, may every obstacle become a vehicle to make us stronger and more determined.**
>
> **Help us to understand the great price we must pay to be molded in the fire and make us willing to stretch for all that we can be for the next generation, so they we can go further than we have ever been and**

do more than we ever thought possible. May the leaders of Your Kingdom have all of the necessary virtues, strengths, character traits, skills and training to make them successful.

In Jesus' precious and wonderful name and for His glory alone, Amen!

WHEN WE HAVE DONE ALL WE KNOW TO DO AND THEN WE TAKE ONE MORE STEP BEYOND OURSELVES, GOD HONORS OUR FAITH!

Chapter 15

Closing Thoughts and Parting Shots on Finishing Well

Mark 12:30-31

> *"And you shall love the LORD your God with all your heart, with all your soul, with all your mind, and with all your strength." This is the first commandment. And the second, like it, is this: "You shall love your neighbor as yourself." There is no other commandment greater than these.*

Wow! If you have read all the way to here, there really isn't much more about leadership that I can tell you. But you can read about leadership all day long and know all the principles and concepts and never step into it. Much of what we experience that creates in us the ability to lead others must be done in the

Spirit. Our greatest need is to be taught by the Spirit and led by the Spirit in this furnace of adversity and affliction, in this place of trial and tribulation—the University of Hard Knocks.

Leadership is not something that can be easily taught or easily learned. It is something that must be lived out and walked out in a place of faith and love.

The great command that the ultimate Leader and CEO of His Church, Jesus of Nazareth, gave us in Mark is, first of all: *"And you shall love the LORD your God with all your heart, with all your soul, with all your mind, and with all your strength,"* and then *"You shall love your neighbor as yourself."* You can do this!

As the prophet Micah revealed, the Lord doesn't ask much of man:

Micah 6:8

> *He has shown you, O mortal, what is good.*
> *And what does the LORD require of you?*
> *To act justly and to love mercy*
> *and to walk humbly with your God.*

I enjoy leading, but if I somehow found myself not to be a godly leader, I would prefer not to lead at all. Otherwise I might lead someone in the wrong direction. I enjoy the quest for success and significance, but what good is it if I gain the whole world and lose my own soul.

I hope that this book challenges you to take a good look inside yourself. I hope it causes you to look back to where you came from, so that you can reach forward to the destiny you were born for and begin *Leading on the Prophetic Edge*.

My closing prayer for you is that the Lord would give you revelation and wisdom and understanding, that He would open your eyes to every opportunity, that He would mightily connect you together with other like-minded individuals, that He would guide you by the power of His Spirit and the power of His love. I pray that He would bless you and your family spiritually, emotionally and financially.

In Jesus' name,
Amen!

MOST MEN, LIKE ALL RIVERS, SEEM TO TAKE THE PATH OF LEAST RESISTANCE! HOW ABOUT YOU?

Bibliography

Much of the teaching and material that I have received prophetically over the years has come as revelation from the Lord. But I would like to acknowledge some whose teachings and writings have had an impact on me and that I gleaned from on my own prophetic journey.

Burford, Bob. *Beyond Half Time: Practical Wisdom for Your Second Half.* Grand Rapids, MI: Zondervan Publishers, 2008

Burford, Bob. *Half Time.* Grand Rapids, MI: Zondervan Publishers, 2009

Connor, Daryl. *Leading on the Edge of Chaos.* Westminster, London: Prentice Hall Press, 2002

Dungy, Tony. *Mentor Leader.* Carol Stream, IL: Tyn-

Bibliography

dale House Publishers, 2010

Hill, Napoleon. *Laws of Success.* Gordonsville, VA: High Roads Media, 2004

Holtz, Lou. *Wins, Losses and Lessons.* New York, NY: William Morrow Publishers, 2006

Iacocca, Lee. *Where Have All the Leaders Gone?* Chicago, IL: Simon and Schuster, 2007

Miller, Tony. *The Journey of Significance.* Orlando, FL: Strong Communications Co., 2003

Peel, Norman Vincent. *The Positive Principles.* Carmel, NY: Guideposts Associates Inc., 1974

Wolfe, Lorin. *Leadership Secrets from the Bible.* New York, NY: MJF Books, 2002

Author Contact Page

You may contact the author in the following ways:

By Email
bro.russ @ eagleworldwide.com

By Phone:
+1 905 308 9991

By Mail:
PO Box 39
Copetown ON L0R1J0
Canada

On Facebook:

facebook.com/eagleworldwide

facebook.com/russ.moyer.52

By visiting his website:
www.EagleWorldwide.com

EAGLE WORLDWIDE RETREAT & REVIVAL CENTRE

SUMMER CAMP TENT REVIVAL

July through August
8 Powerful Weeks of Revival
Every Night @ 7:00pm

Specialty Schools
School of the Prophets
School of Freedom and Healing
School of the Supernatural

Location: 976 Hwy 52 Copetown ON L0R 1J0
Call for more details 905 308 9991
www.EagleWorldwide.com

WINTER CAMP REVIVAL GLORY

February/March
10 Powerful Days of Revival Glory
Every Night @ 7:00pm

Specialty Schools
School of the Prophets

The Dwelling Place
7895 Pensacola Blvd Pensacola FL 32534
Call for more details 850 473 8255
www.TheDwellingPlaceChurch.org

EAGLE WORLDWIDE NETWORK

CREDENTIALING & SPIRITUALLY COVERING

Ministers
Marketplace Ministers
Traveling & Itinerant Ministers
Missionaries
Churches
Church Networks
Home Churches
Outreach Ministries
And more...

GOVERNING OFFICIAL
PASTOR MAVE MOYER

NETWORK COORDINATOR
PASTOR JOANNA ADAMS

CREDENTIALS AVAILABLE

Certified Practical Minister
Licensed Minister
Ordained Minister

OFFICE@EAGLEWORLDWIDE.COM